STAR WARS ADVENTURES

PRINCESS LEIA AND THE ROYAL RANSOM

D0104306

Designer
David Nestelle

Assistant Editor
Freddye Lins

Editor
Randy Stradley

Publisher
Mike Richardson

special thanks to Elaine Mederer, Jann Moorhead, David Anderman,
Leland Chee, Sue Rostoni, and Carol Roeder at Lucas Licensing

STAR WARS ADVENTURES: PRINCESS LEIA AND THE ROYAL RANSOM

Published by
Dark Horse Books
A division of Dark Horse Comics, Inc.
10956 SE Main Street
Milwaukie, OR 97222

darkhorse.com
starwars.com

To find a comics shop in your area, call the Comic Shop Locator Service toll-free at 1-888-266-4226

First edition: July 2009
ISBN 978-1-59582-147-8

10 9 8 7 6 5 4 3 2 1
Printed in China

STAR WARS ADVENTURES

PRINCESS LEIA AND THE ROYAL RANSOM

Script **Jeremy Barlow**

Art **Carlo Soriano**

Colors **Michael Atiyeh**

Lettering **Michael Heisler**

Cover art **Sean McNally**

Dark Horse Books®

THIS STORY TAKES PLACE APPROXIMATELY ONE YEAR BEFORE STAR WARS: THE EMPIRE STRIKES BACK.

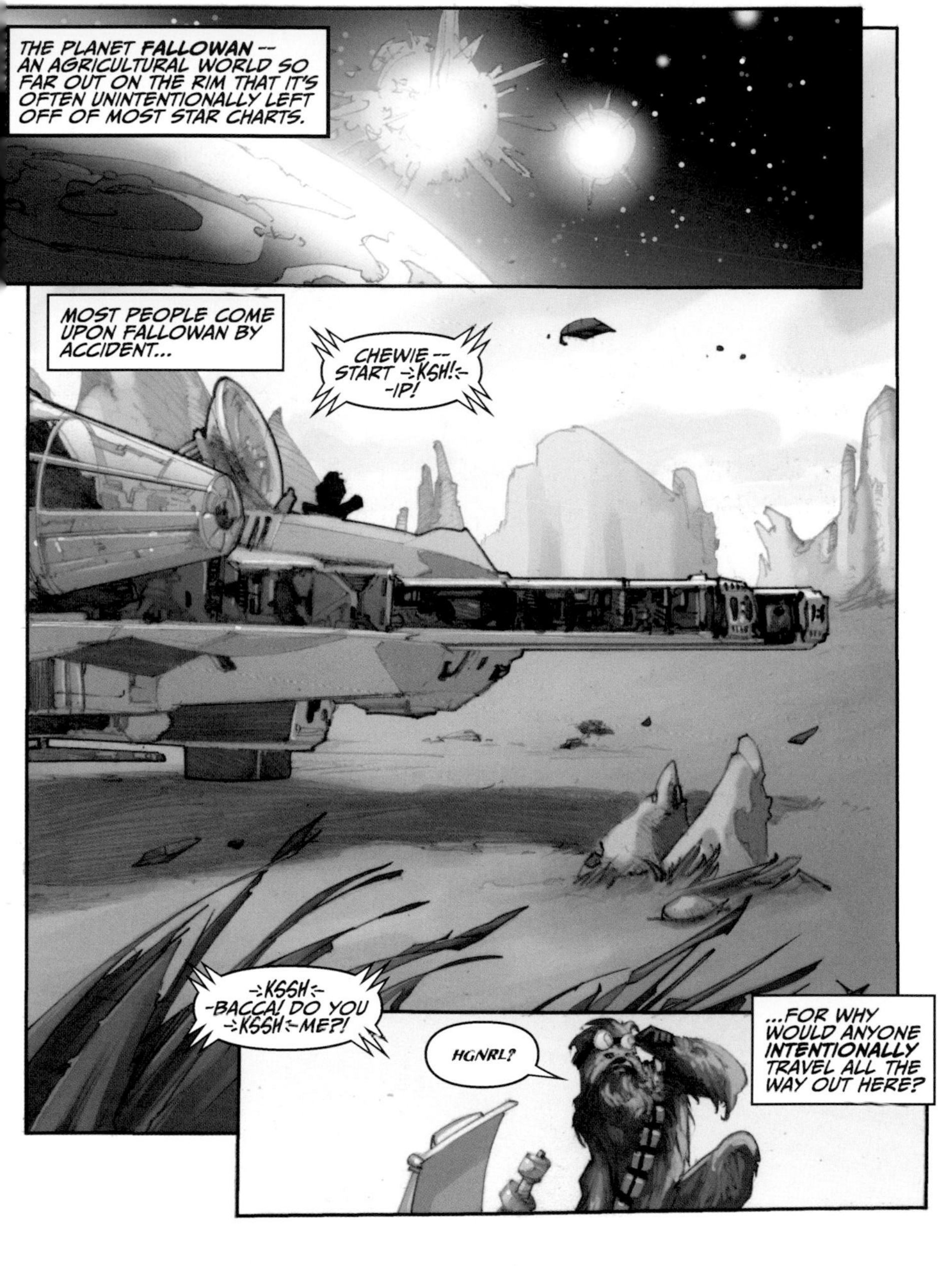

THE PLANET FALLOWAN -- AN AGRICULTURAL WORLD SO FAR OUT ON THE RIM THAT IT'S OFTEN UNINTENTIONALLY LEFT OFF OF MOST STAR CHARTS.
MOST PEOPLE COME UPON FALLOWAN BY ACCIDENT...
CHEWIE -- START -KSH!- -IP!
-KSSH- -BACCA! DO YOU -KSSH- ME?!
HGNRL?
...FOR WHY WOULD ANYONE INTENTIONALLY TRAVEL ALL THE WAY OUT HERE?

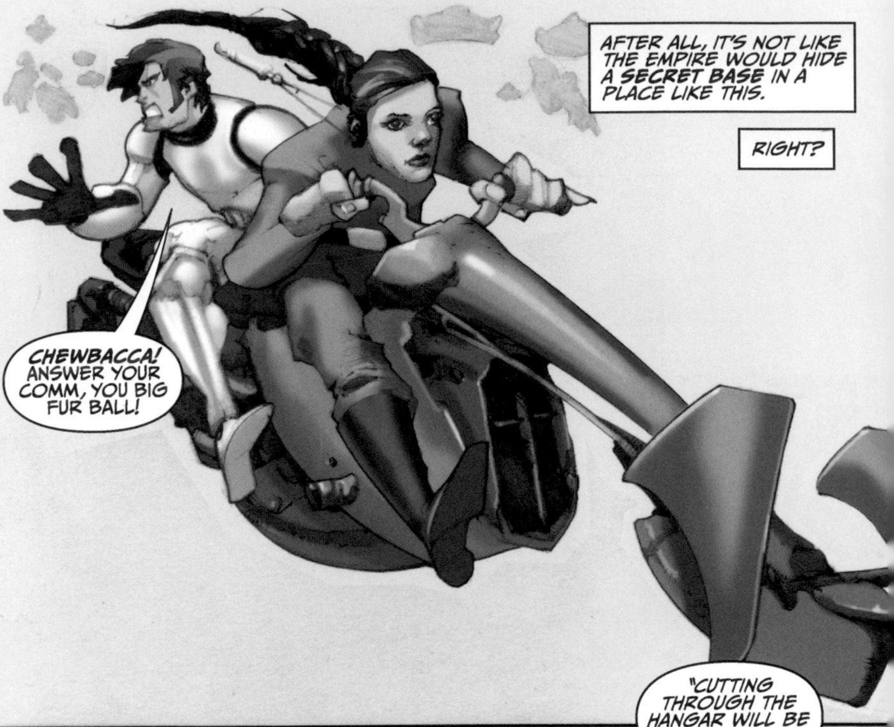
AFTER ALL, IT'S NOT LIKE THE EMPIRE WOULD HIDE A **SECRET BASE** IN A PLACE LIKE THIS.
RIGHT?
CHEWBACCA! ANSWER YOUR COMM, YOU BIG FUR BALL!

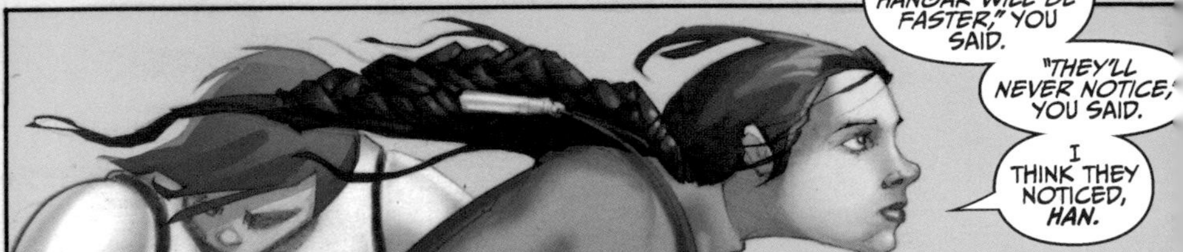
"CUTTING THROUGH THE HANGAR WILL BE FASTER," YOU SAID.
"THEY'LL NEVER NOTICE," YOU SAID.
I THINK THEY NOTICED, **HAN.**

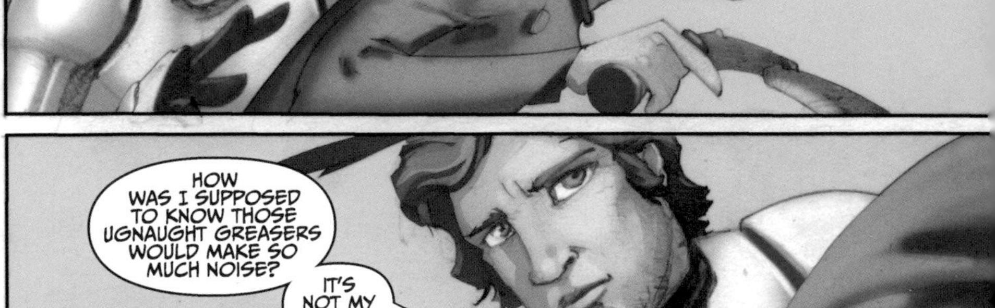
HOW WAS I SUPPOSED TO KNOW THOSE UGNAUGHT GREASERS WOULD MAKE SO MUCH NOISE?
IT'S NOT MY FAULT!

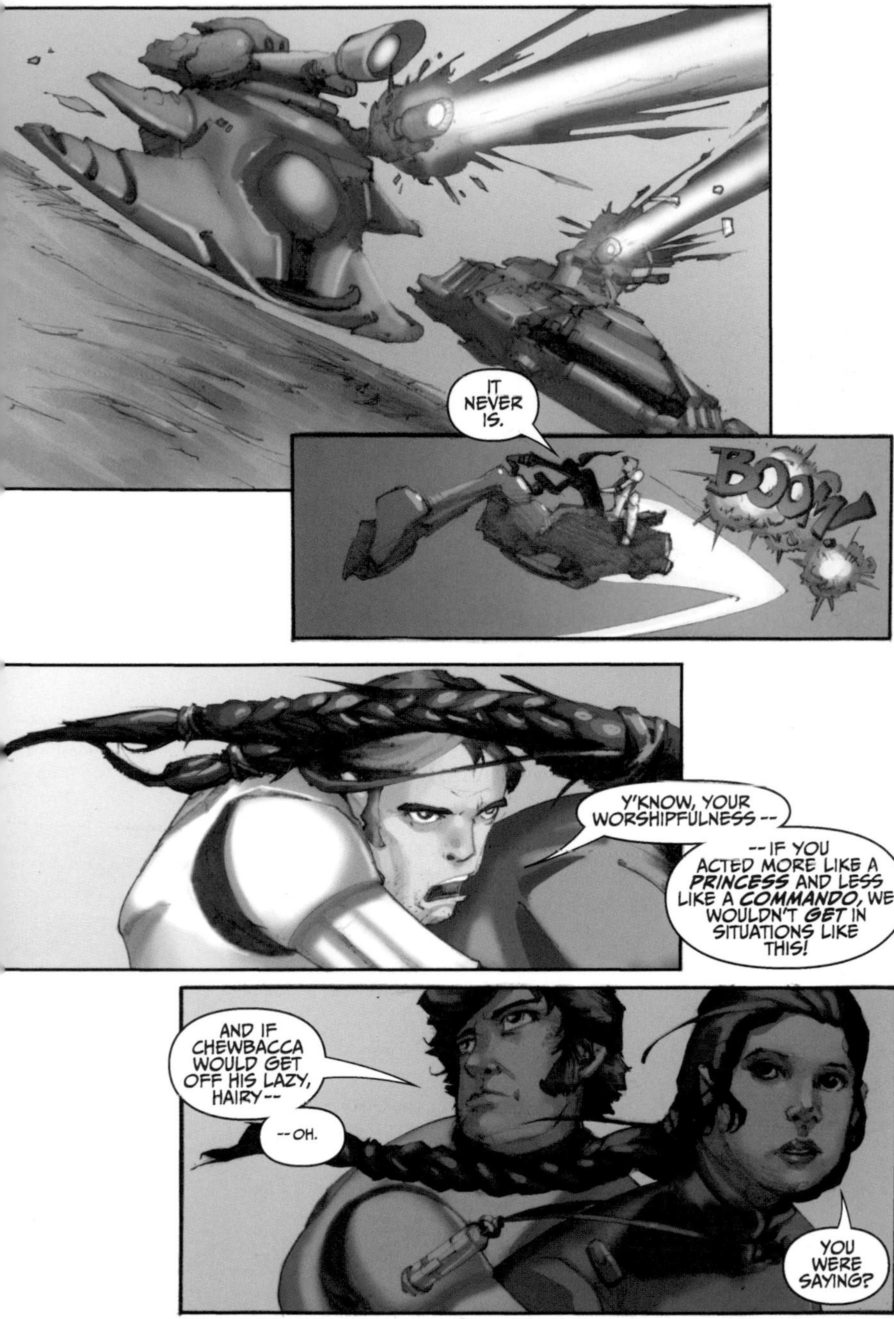
IT NEVER IS.
BOOM!
Y'KNOW, YOUR WORSHIPFULNESS --
-- IF YOU ACTED MORE LIKE A *PRINCESS* AND LESS LIKE A *COMMANDO*, WE WOULDN'T *GET* IN SITUATIONS LIKE THIS!
AND IF CHEWBACCA WOULD GET OFF HIS LAZY, HAIRY--
--OH.
YOU WERE SAYING?

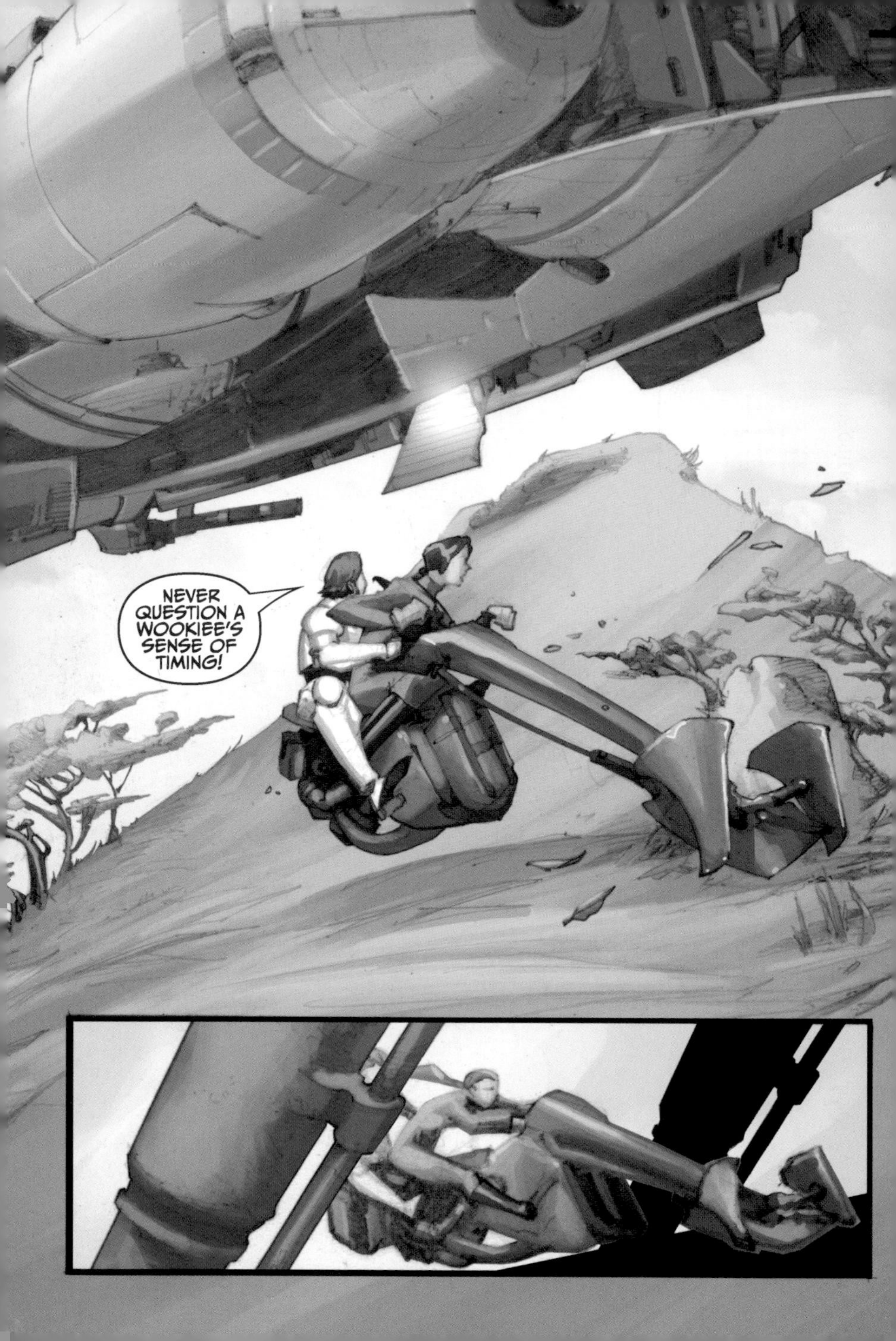
NEVER QUESTION A WOOKIEE'S SENSE OF TIMING!

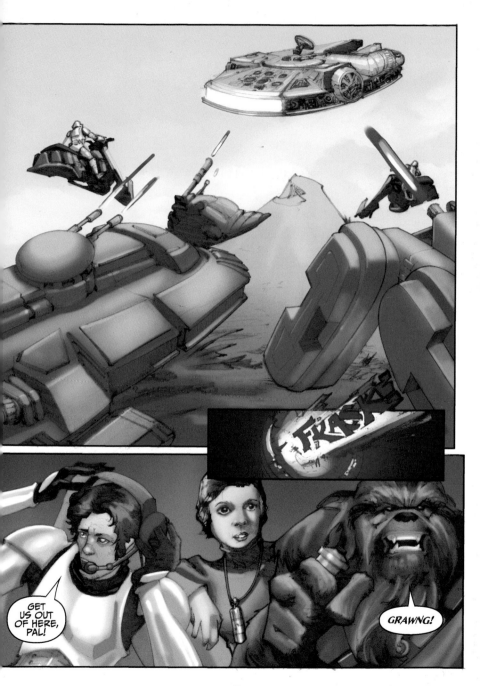

GET US OUT OF HERE, PAL!

FRASK!

GRAWNG!

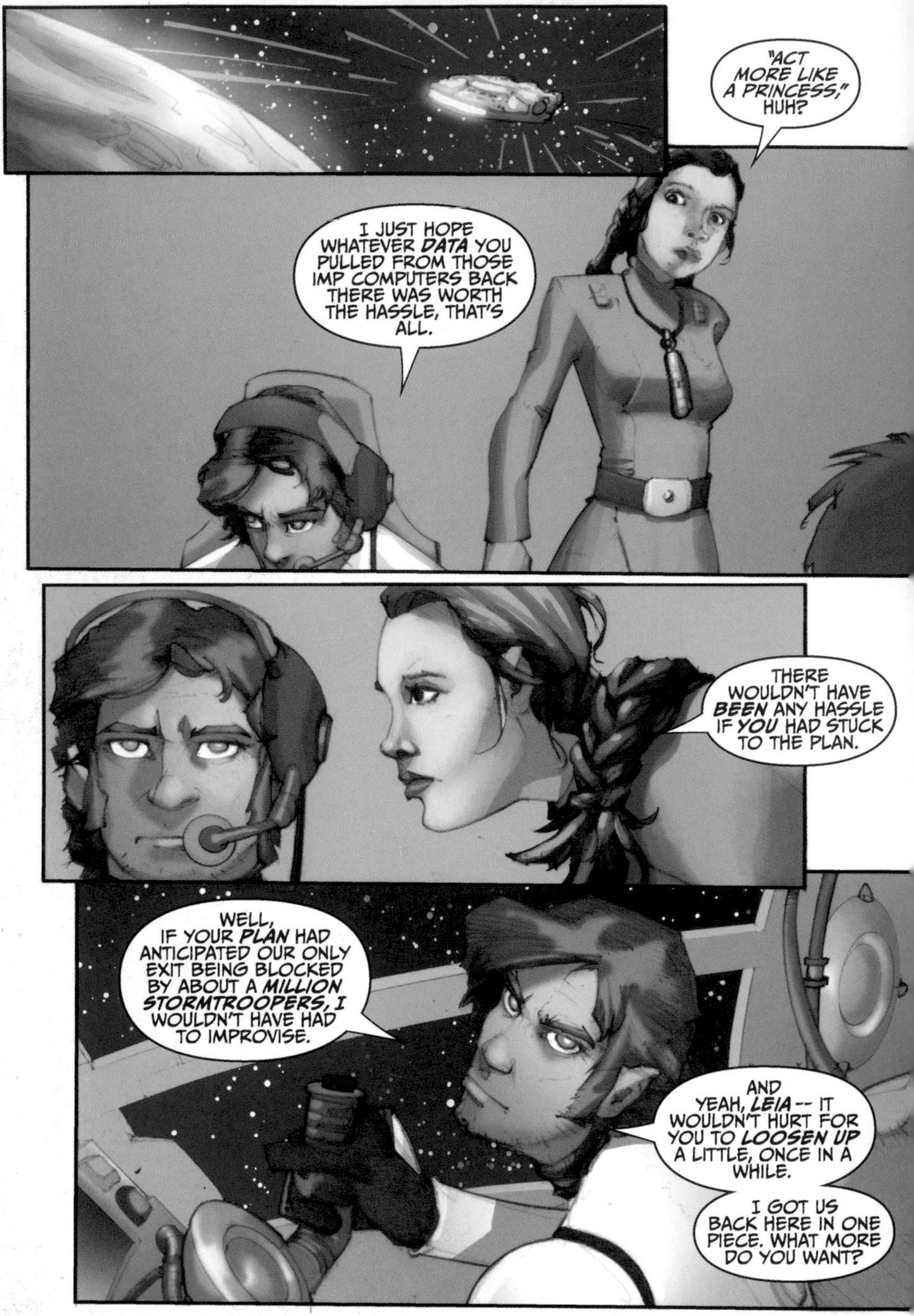
"ACT MORE LIKE A PRINCESS," HUH?
I JUST HOPE WHATEVER DATA YOU PULLED FROM THOSE IMP COMPUTERS BACK THERE WAS WORTH THE HASSLE, THAT'S ALL.
THERE WOULDN'T HAVE BEEN ANY HASSLE IF YOU HAD STUCK TO THE PLAN.
WELL, IF YOUR PLAN HAD ANTICIPATED OUR ONLY EXIT BEING BLOCKED BY ABOUT A MILLION STORMTROOPERS, I WOULDN'T HAVE HAD TO IMPROVISE.
AND YEAH, LEIA -- IT WOULDN'T HURT FOR YOU TO LOOSEN UP A LITTLE, ONCE IN A WHILE.
I GOT US BACK HERE IN ONE PIECE. WHAT MORE DO YOU WANT?

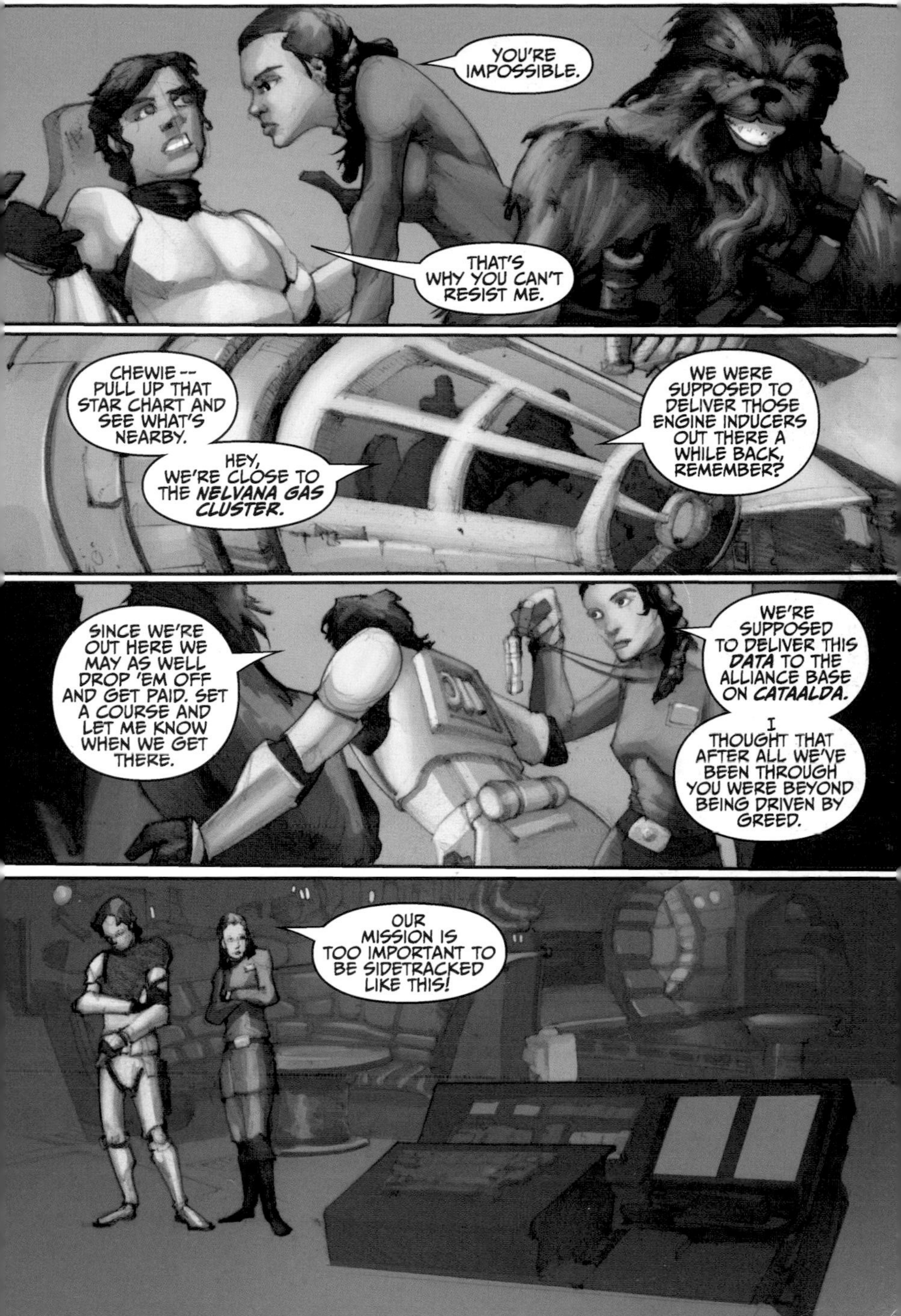
YOU'RE IMPOSSIBLE.
THAT'S WHY YOU CAN'T RESIST ME.
CHEWIE -- PULL UP THAT STAR CHART AND SEE WHAT'S NEARBY.
HEY, WE'RE CLOSE TO THE NELVANA GAS CLUSTER.
WE WERE SUPPOSED TO DELIVER THOSE ENGINE INDUCERS OUT THERE A WHILE BACK, REMEMBER?
SINCE WE'RE OUT HERE WE MAY AS WELL DROP 'EM OFF AND GET PAID. SET A COURSE AND LET ME KNOW WHEN WE GET THERE.
WE'RE SUPPOSED TO DELIVER THIS DATA TO THE ALLIANCE BASE ON CATAALDA.
I THOUGHT THAT AFTER ALL WE'VE BEEN THROUGH YOU WERE BEYOND BEING DRIVEN BY GREED.
OUR MISSION IS TOO IMPORTANT TO BE SIDETRACKED LIKE THIS!

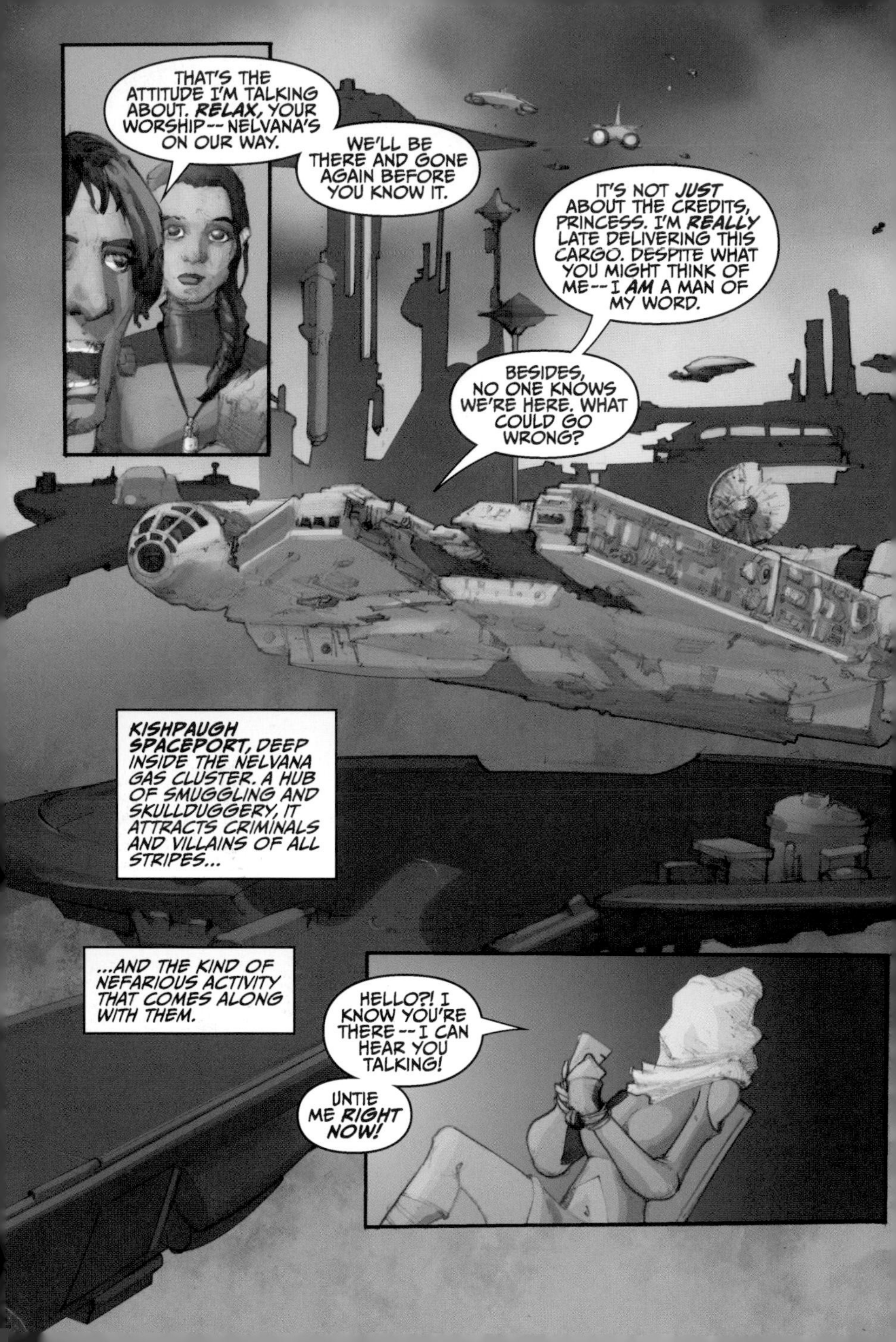
THAT'S THE ATTITUDE I'M TALKING ABOUT. RELAX, YOUR WORSHIP--NELVANA'S ON OUR WAY.
WE'LL BE THERE AND GONE AGAIN BEFORE YOU KNOW IT.
IT'S NOT JUST ABOUT THE CREDITS, PRINCESS. I'M REALLY LATE DELIVERING THIS CARGO. DESPITE WHAT YOU MIGHT THINK OF ME--I AM A MAN OF MY WORD.
BESIDES, NO ONE KNOWS WE'RE HERE. WHAT COULD GO WRONG?
KISHPAUGH SPACEPORT, DEEP INSIDE THE NELVANA GAS CLUSTER. A HUB OF SMUGGLING AND SKULLDUGGERY, IT ATTRACTS CRIMINALS AND VILLAINS OF ALL STRIPES...
...AND THE KIND OF NEFARIOUS ACTIVITY THAT COMES ALONG WITH THEM.
HELLO?! I KNOW YOU'RE THERE--I CAN HEAR YOU TALKING!
UNTIE ME RIGHT NOW!

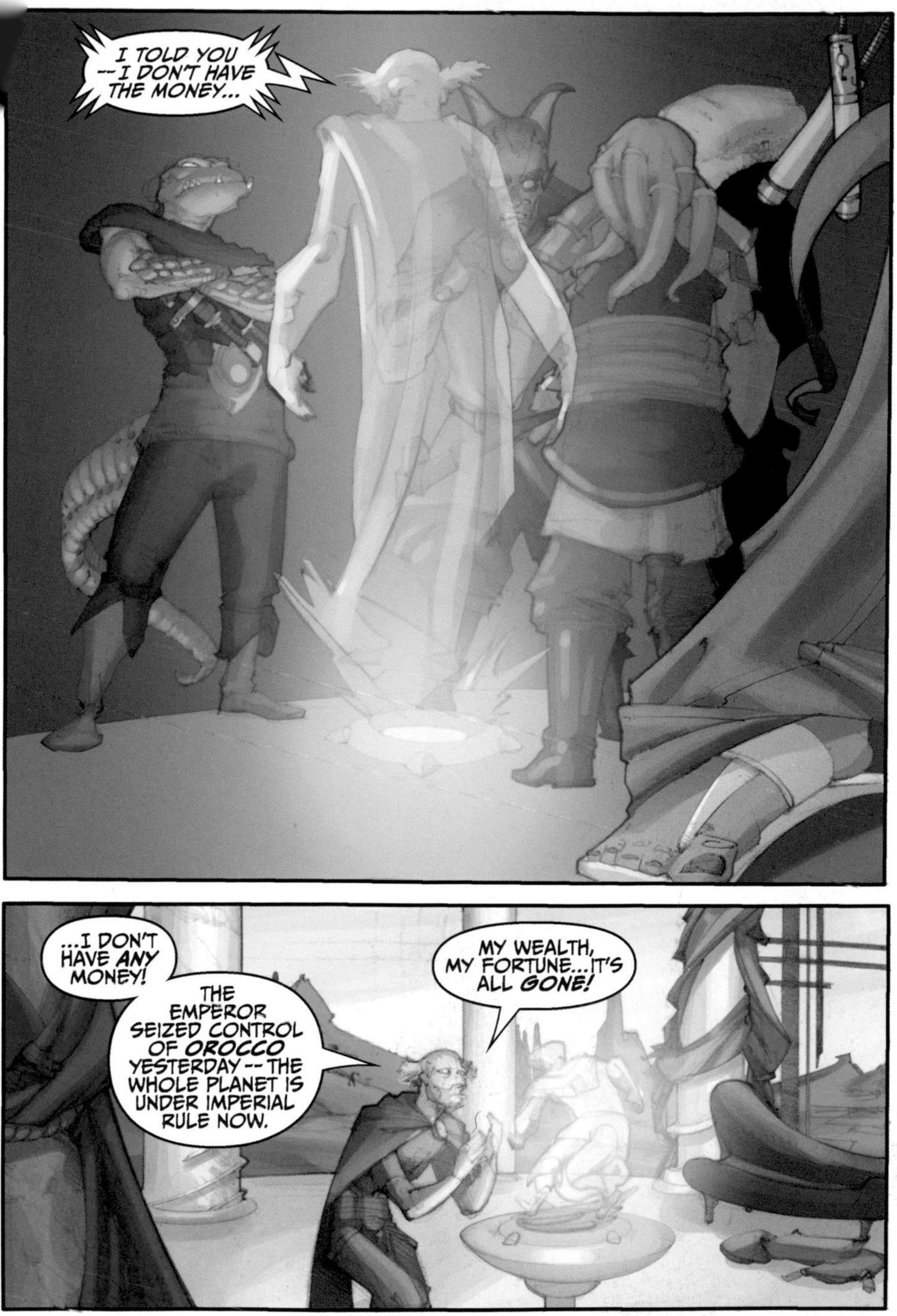
I TOLD YOU --I DON'T HAVE THE MONEY...
...I DON'T HAVE ANY MONEY!
THE EMPEROR SEIZED CONTROL OF OROCCO YESTERDAY -- THE WHOLE PLANET IS UNDER IMPERIAL RULE NOW.
MY WEALTH, MY FORTUNE...IT'S ALL GONE!

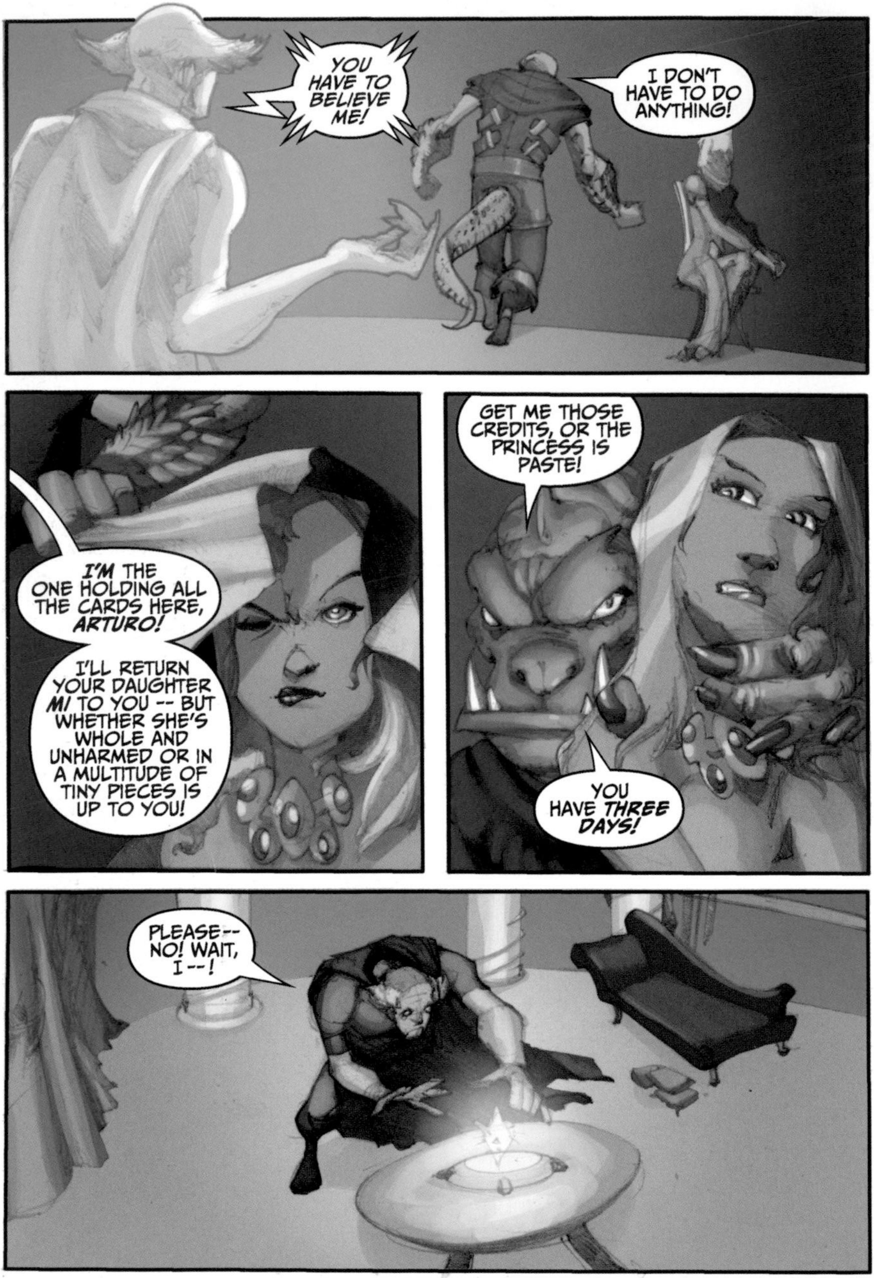
YOU HAVE TO BELIEVE ME!
I DON'T HAVE TO DO ANYTHING!
I'M THE ONE HOLDING ALL THE CARDS HERE, ARTURO!
I'LL RETURN YOUR DAUGHTER MI TO YOU -- BUT WHETHER SHE'S WHOLE AND UNHARMED OR IN A MULTITUDE OF TINY PIECES IS UP TO YOU!
GET ME THOSE CREDITS, OR THE PRINCESS IS PASTE!
YOU HAVE THREE DAYS!
PLEASE-- NO! WAIT, I--!

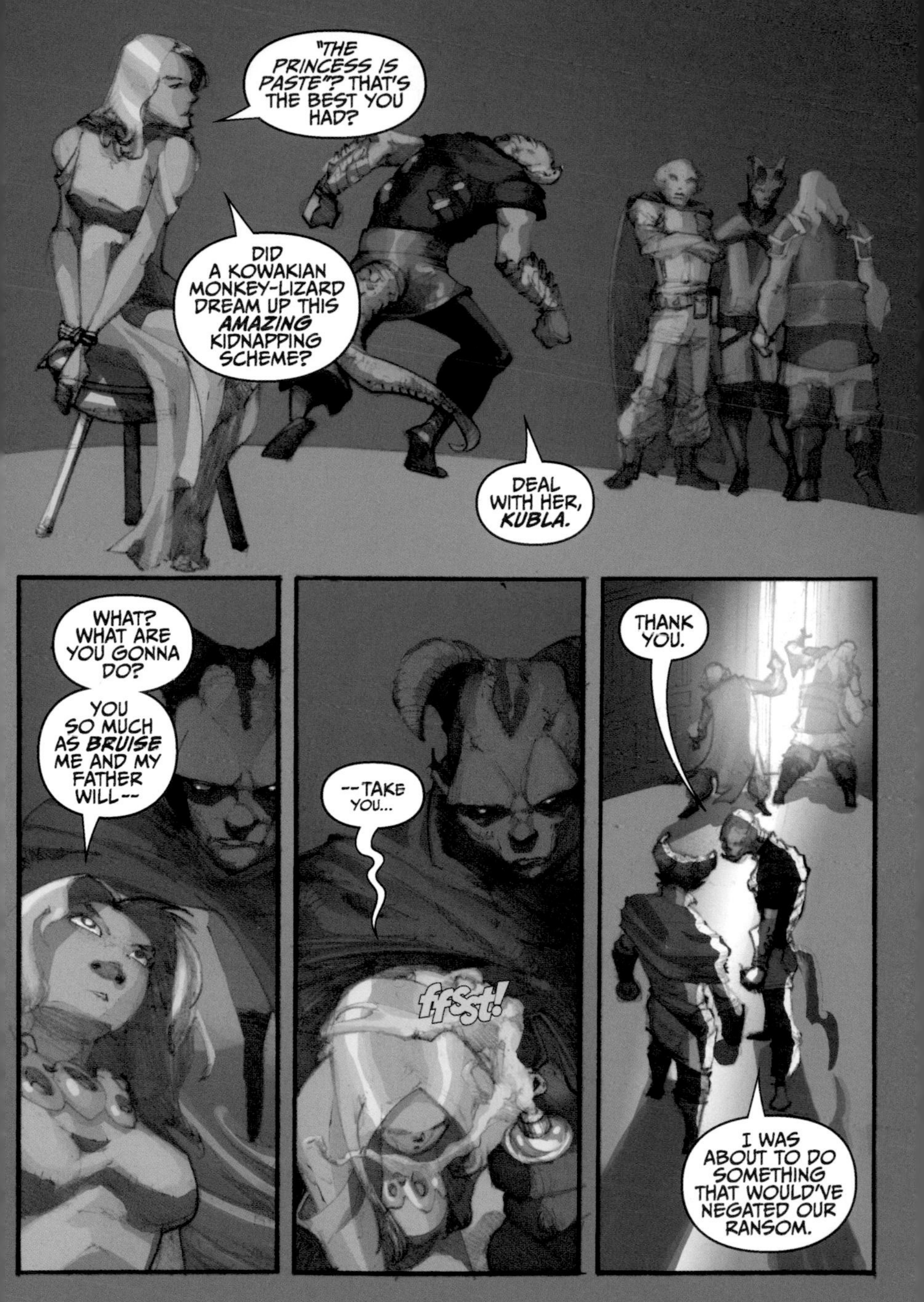
"THE PRINCESS IS PASTE"? THAT'S THE BEST YOU HAD?
DID A KOWAKIAN MONKEY-LIZARD DREAM UP THIS *AMAZING* KIDNAPPING SCHEME?
DEAL WITH HER, *KUBLA.*
WHAT? WHAT ARE YOU GONNA DO?
YOU SO MUCH AS *BRUISE* ME AND MY FATHER WILL--
--TAKE YOU...
ffst!
THANK YOU.
I WAS ABOUT TO DO SOMETHING THAT WOULD'VE NEGATED OUR RANSOM.

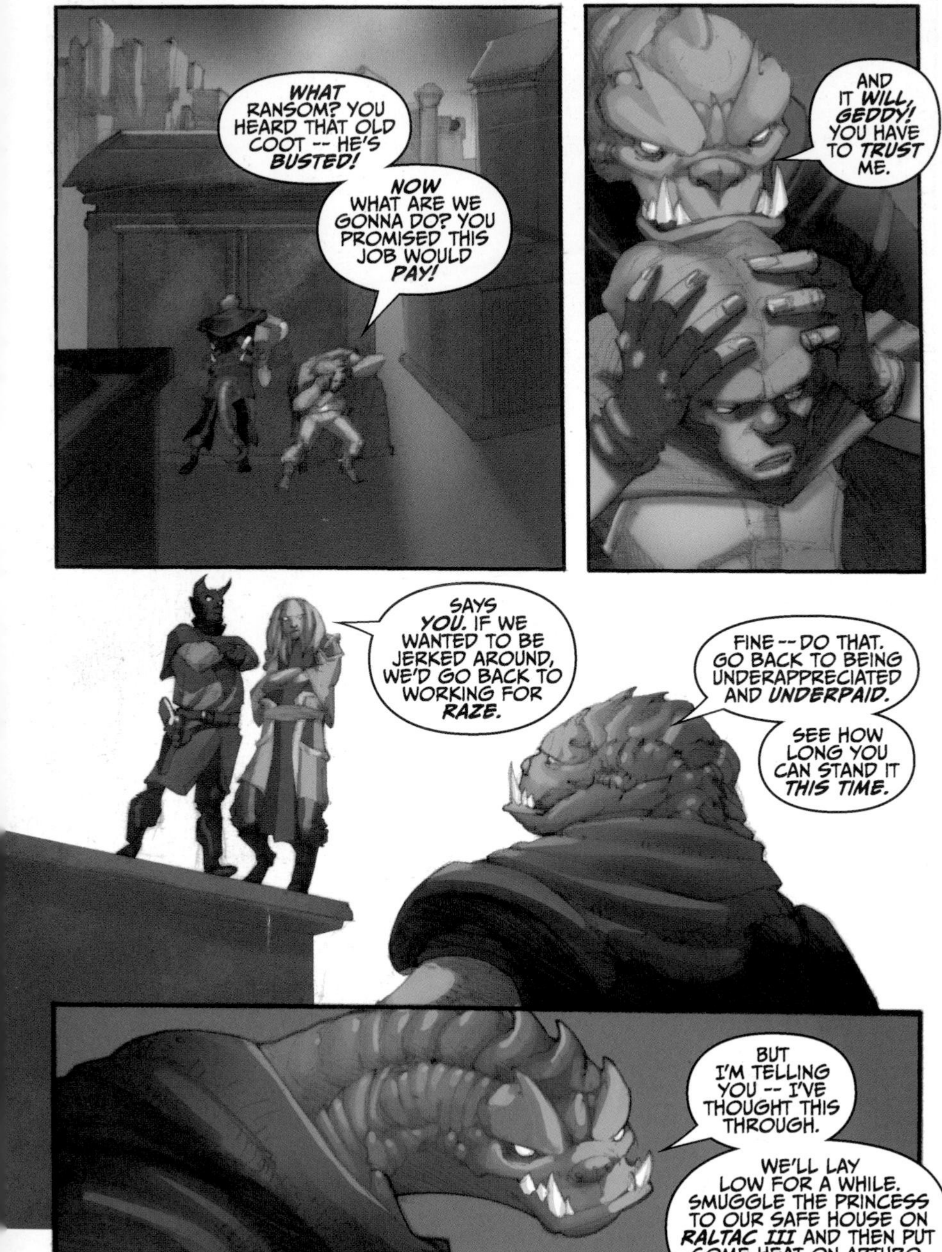
WHAT RANSOM? YOU HEARD THAT OLD COOT -- HE'S BUSTED!
NOW WHAT ARE WE GONNA DO? YOU PROMISED THIS JOB WOULD PAY!
AND IT WILL, GEDDY! YOU HAVE TO TRUST ME.
SAYS YOU. IF WE WANTED TO BE JERKED AROUND, WE'D GO BACK TO WORKING FOR RAZE.
FINE -- DO THAT. GO BACK TO BEING UNDERAPPRECIATED AND UNDERPAID.
SEE HOW LONG YOU CAN STAND IT THIS TIME.
BUT I'M TELLING YOU -- I'VE THOUGHT THIS THROUGH.
WE'LL LAY LOW FOR A WHILE. SMUGGLE THE PRINCESS TO OUR SAFE HOUSE ON RALTAC III AND THEN PUT SOME HEAT ON ARTURO. HE'LL PAY UP-- YOU'LL SEE.

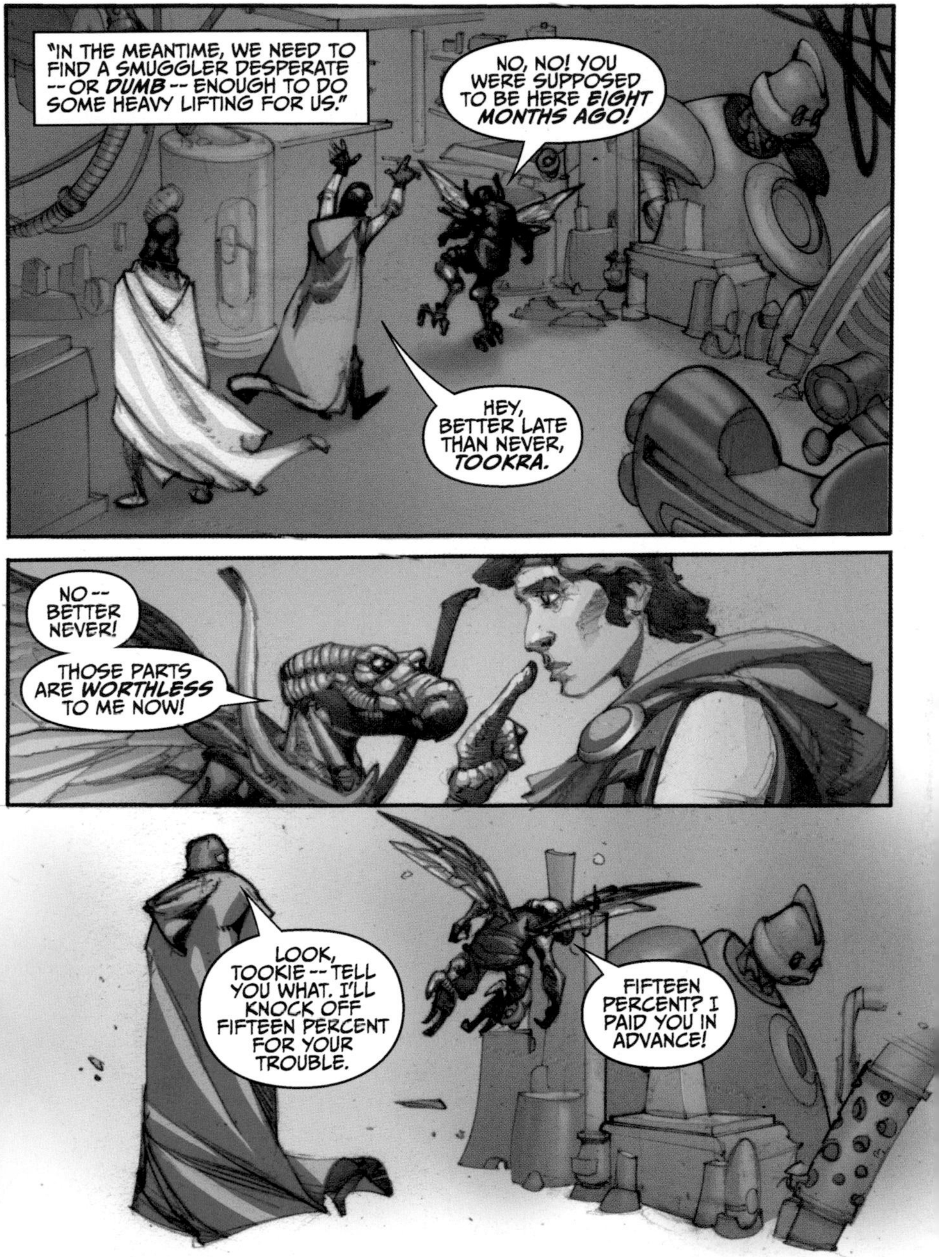
"IN THE MEANTIME, WE NEED TO FIND A SMUGGLER DESPERATE --OR DUMB-- ENOUGH TO DO SOME HEAVY LIFTING FOR US."
NO, NO! YOU WERE SUPPOSED TO BE HERE EIGHT MONTHS AGO!
HEY, BETTER LATE THAN NEVER, TOOKRA.
NO-- BETTER NEVER!
THOSE PARTS ARE WORTHLESS TO ME NOW!
LOOK, TOOKIE--TELL YOU WHAT. I'LL KNOCK OFF FIFTEEN PERCENT FOR YOUR TROUBLE.
FIFTEEN PERCENT? I PAID YOU IN ADVANCE!

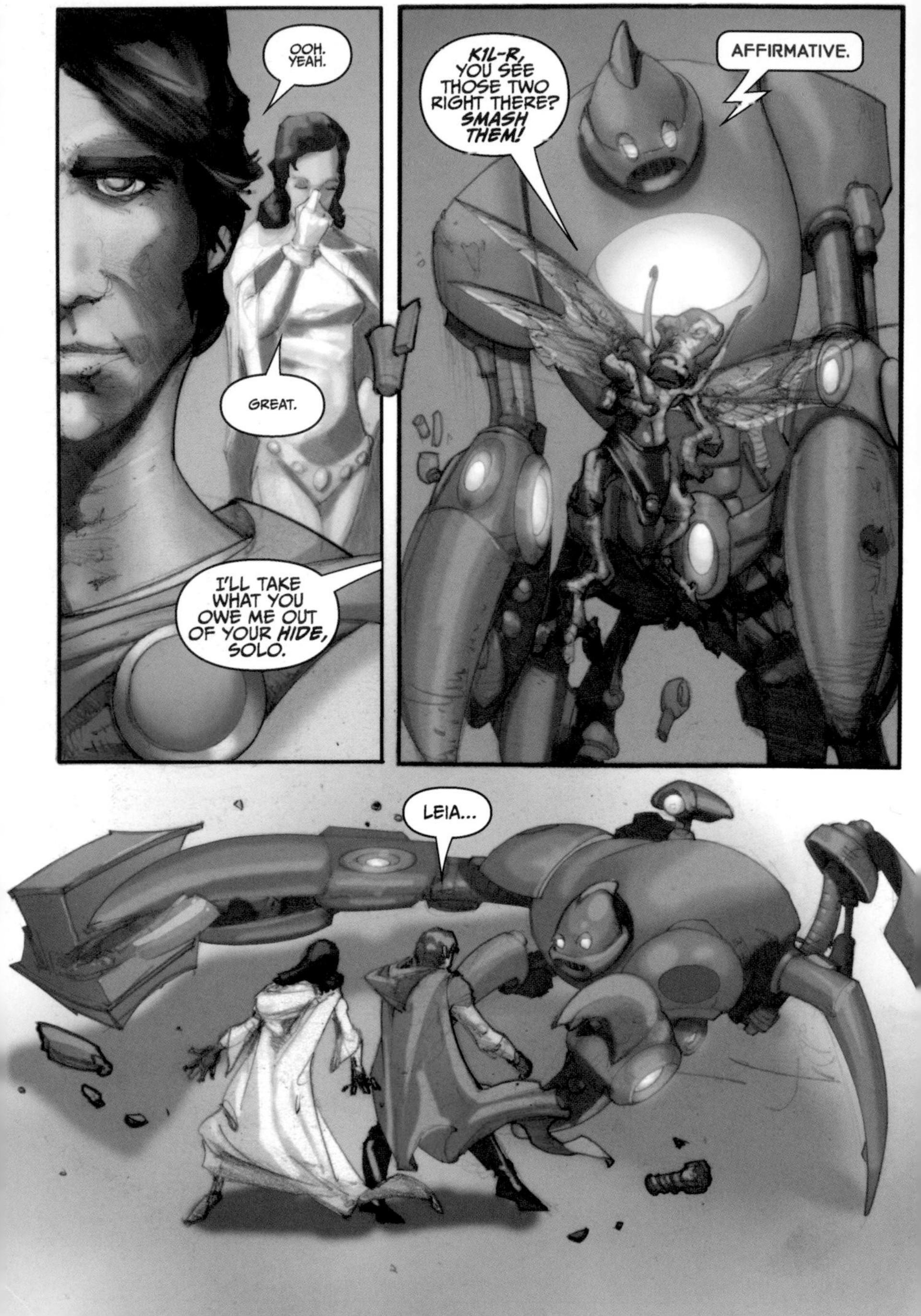
OOH. YEAH.
GREAT.
I'LL TAKE WHAT YOU OWE ME OUT OF YOUR *HIDE*, SOLO.
KIL-R, YOU SEE THOSE TWO RIGHT THERE? *SMASH THEM!*
AFFIRMATIVE.
LEIA...

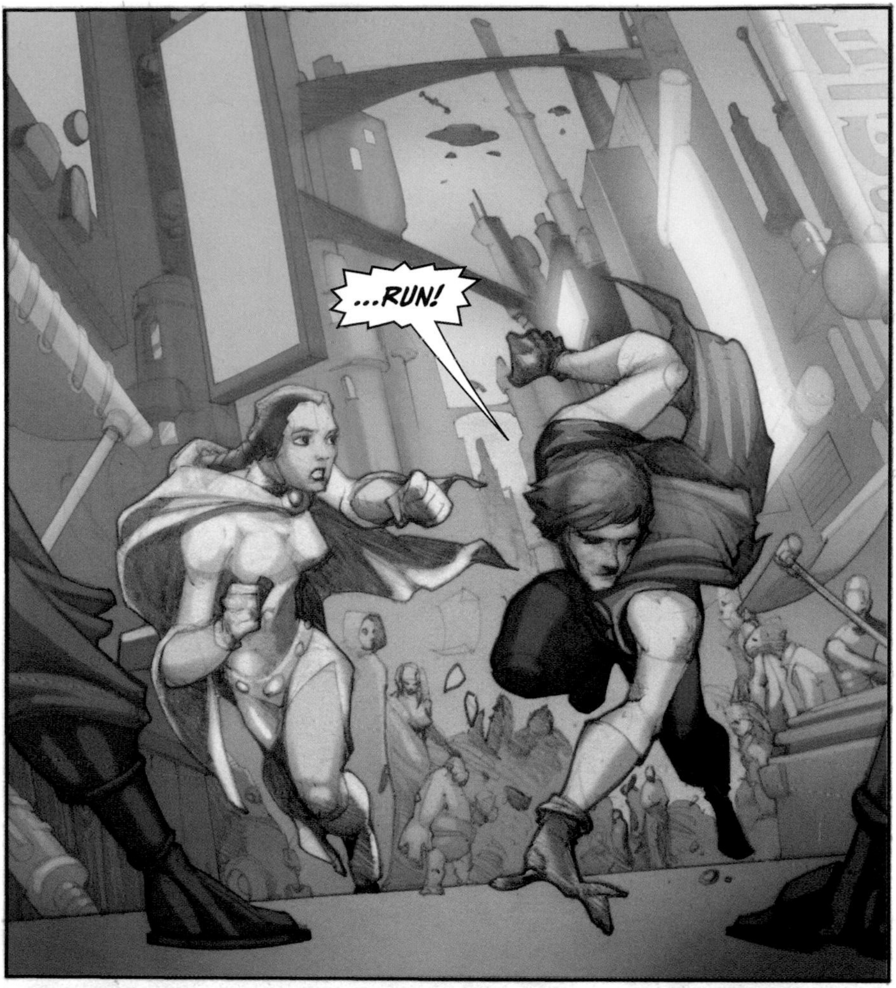
...RUN!

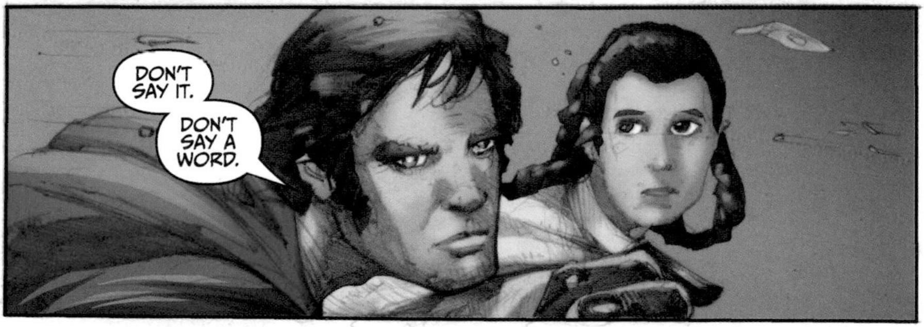
DON'T SAY IT.
DON'T SAY A WORD.

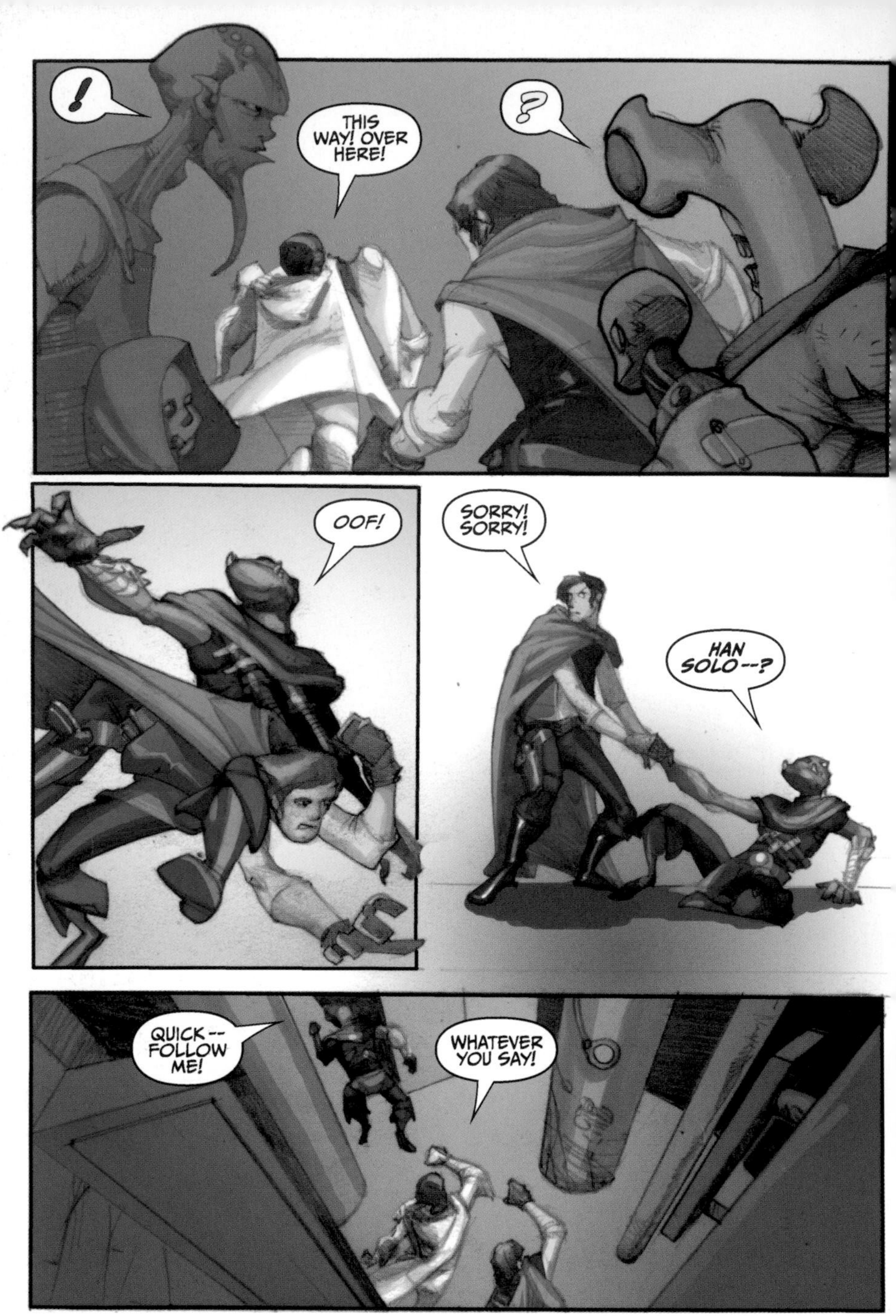
!
THIS WAY! OVER HERE!
?
OOF!
SORRY! SORRY!
HAN SOLO--?
QUICK--FOLLOW ME!
WHATEVER YOU SAY!

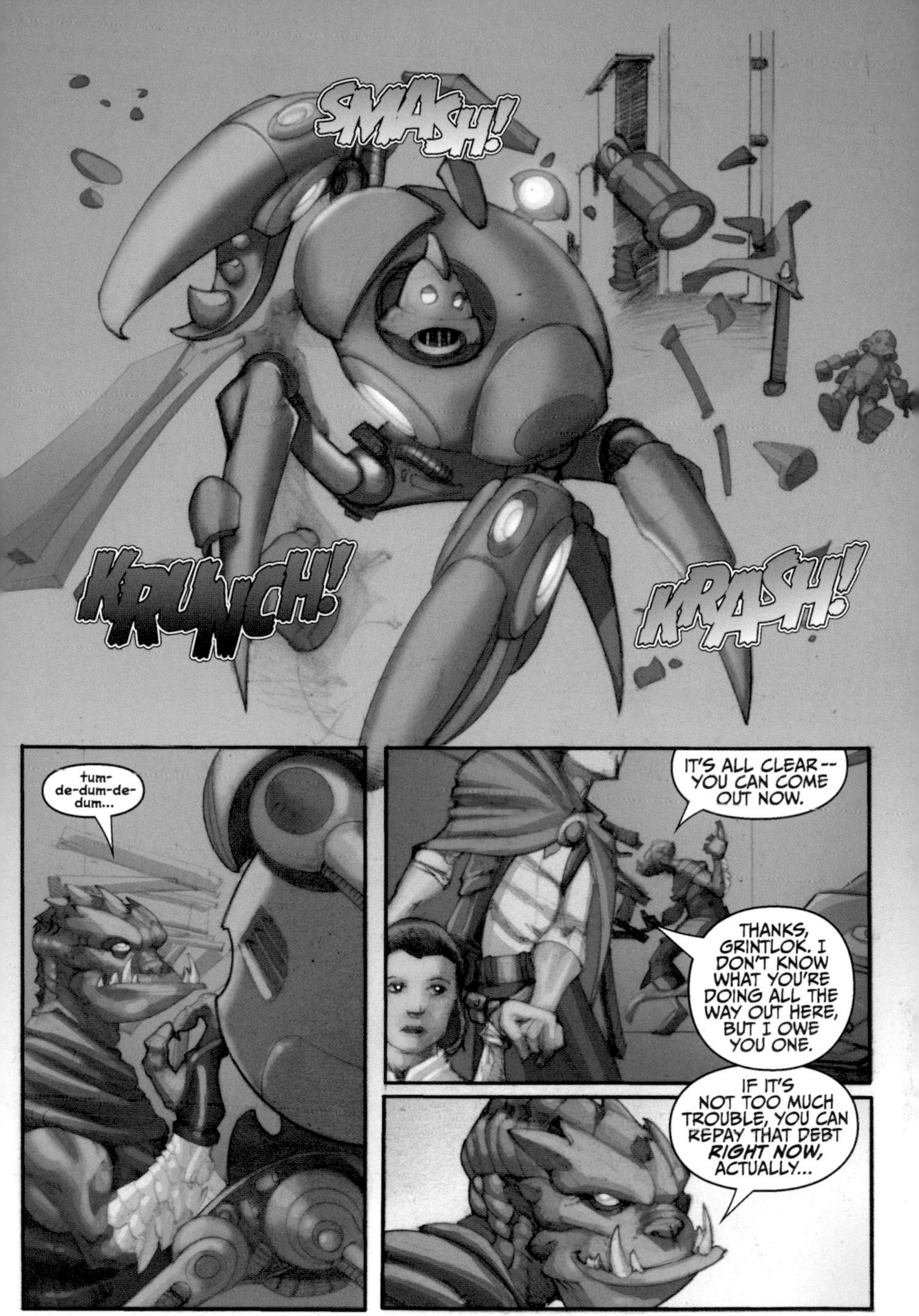
SMASH!
KRUNCH!
KRASH!
tum-de-dum-de-dum...
IT'S ALL CLEAR-- YOU CAN COME OUT NOW.
THANKS, GRINTLOK. I DON'T KNOW WHAT YOU'RE DOING ALL THE WAY OUT HERE, BUT I OWE YOU ONE.
IF IT'S NOT TOO MUCH TROUBLE, YOU CAN REPAY THAT DEBT ***RIGHT NOW,*** ACTUALLY...

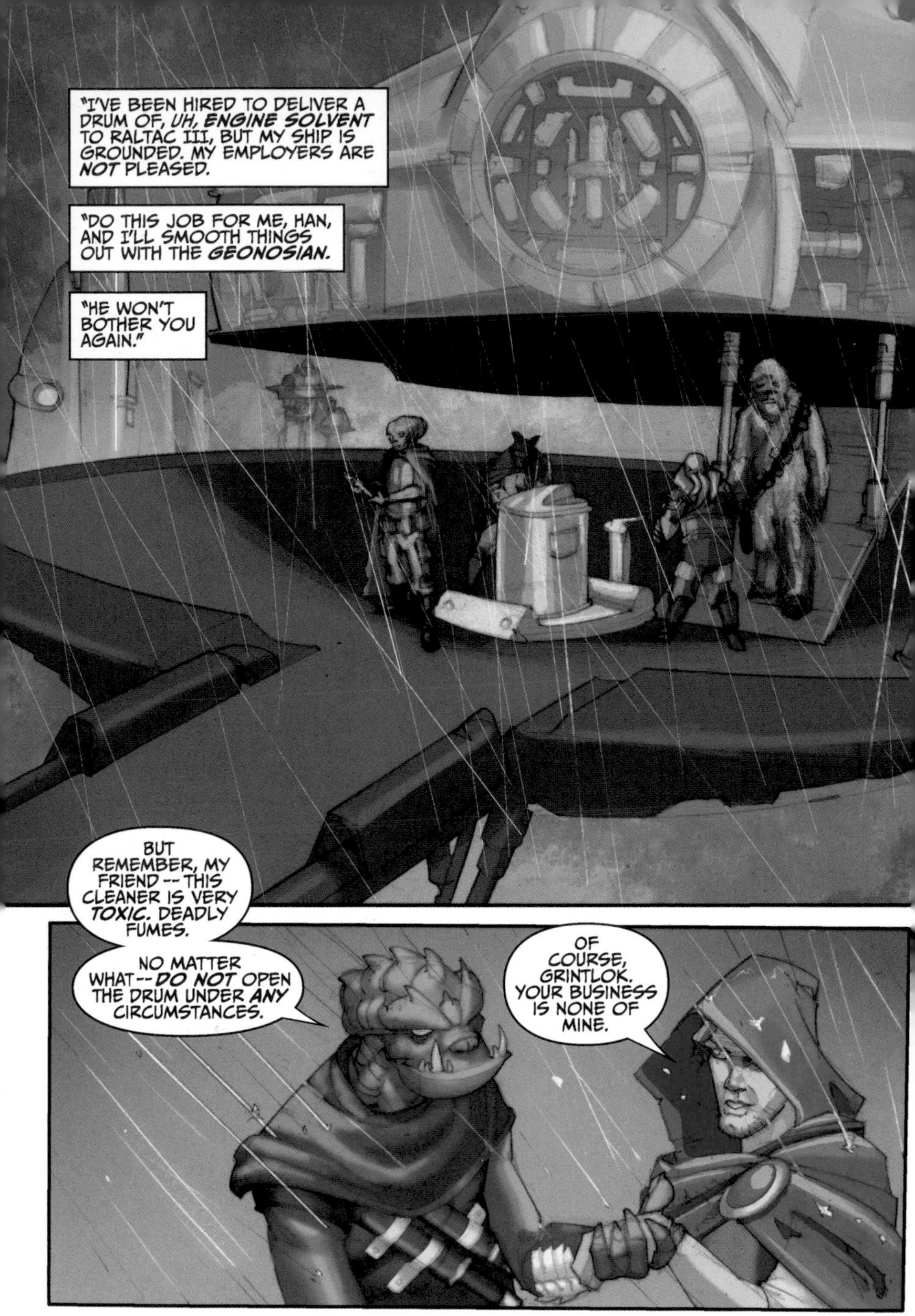
"I'VE BEEN HIRED TO DELIVER A DRUM OF, UH, ENGINE SOLVENT TO RALTAC III, BUT MY SHIP IS GROUNDED. MY EMPLOYERS ARE NOT PLEASED.
"DO THIS JOB FOR ME, HAN, AND I'LL SMOOTH THINGS OUT WITH THE GEONOSIAN.
"HE WON'T BOTHER YOU AGAIN."
BUT REMEMBER, MY FRIEND -- THIS CLEANER IS VERY TOXIC. DEADLY FUMES.
NO MATTER WHAT--DO NOT OPEN THE DRUM UNDER ANY CIRCUMSTANCES.
OF COURSE, GRINTLOK. YOUR BUSINESS IS NONE OF MINE.

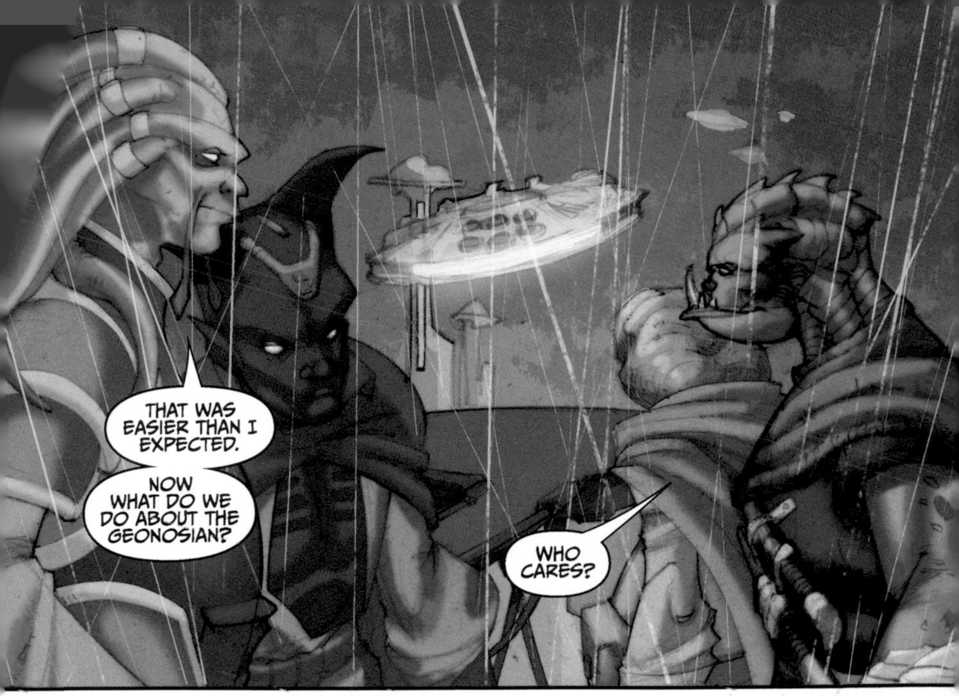
THAT WAS EASIER THAN I EXPECTED.
NOW WHAT DO WE DO ABOUT THE GEONOSIAN?
WHO CARES?

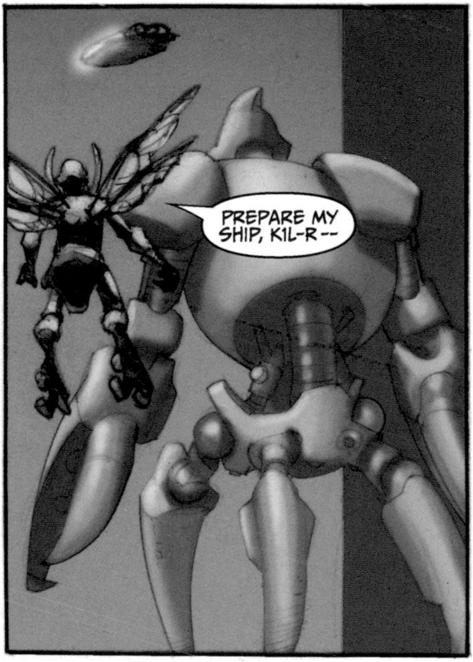
PREPARE MY SHIP, KIL-R --

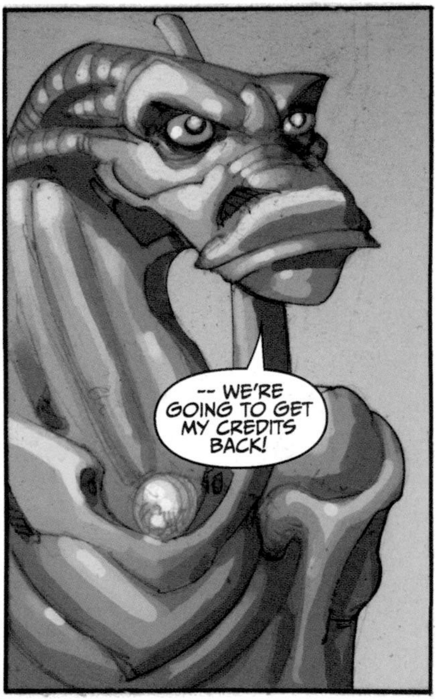
-- WE'RE GOING TO GET MY CREDITS BACK!

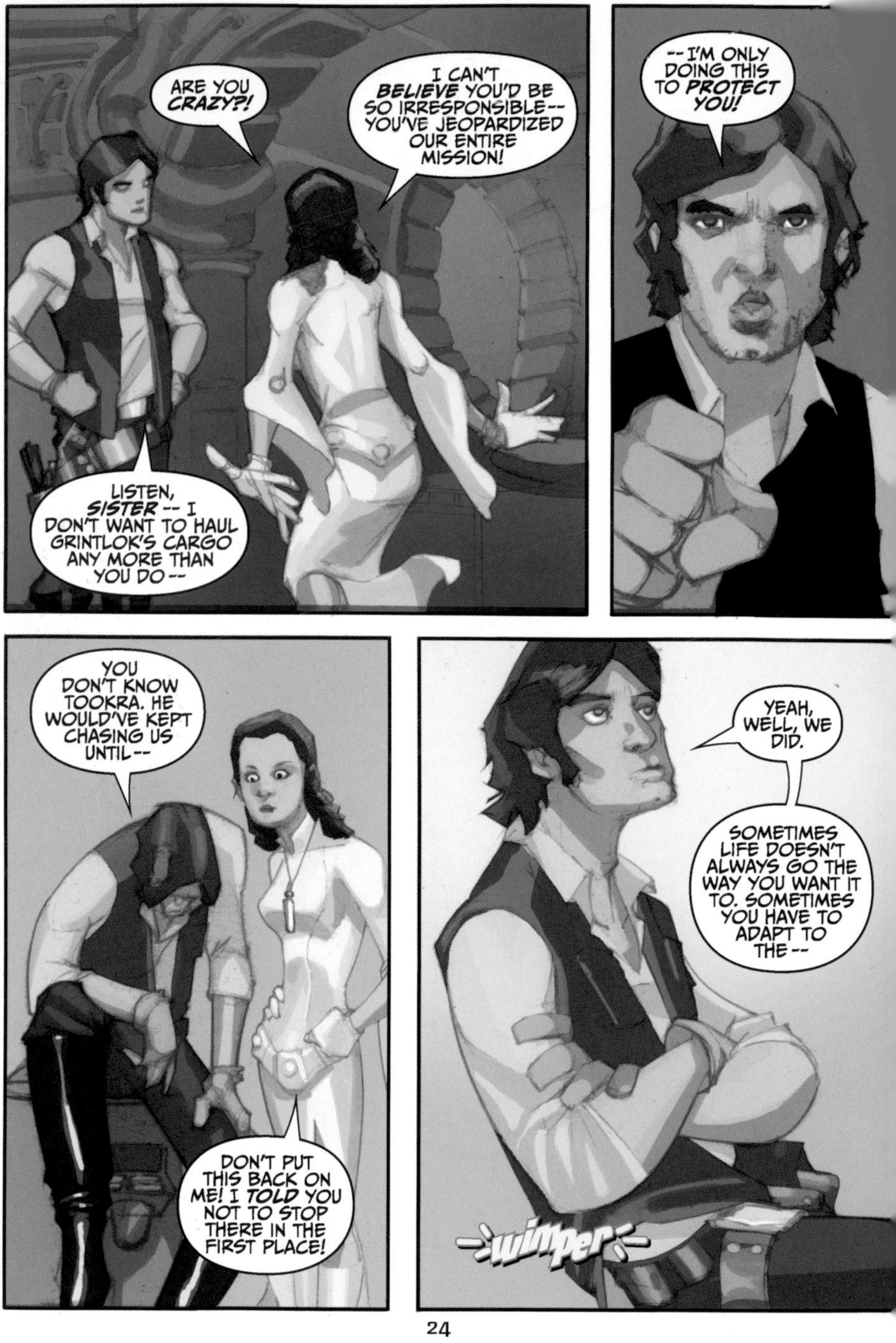
ARE YOU CRAZY?!
I CAN'T BELIEVE YOU'D BE SO IRRESPONSIBLE-- YOU'VE JEOPARDIZED OUR ENTIRE MISSION!
LISTEN, SISTER -- I DON'T WANT TO HAUL GRINTLOK'S CARGO ANY MORE THAN YOU DO --
-- I'M ONLY DOING THIS TO PROTECT YOU!
YOU DON'T KNOW TOOKRA. HE WOULD'VE KEPT CHASING US UNTIL--
DON'T PUT THIS BACK ON ME! I TOLD YOU NOT TO STOP THERE IN THE FIRST PLACE!
YEAH, WELL, WE DID.
SOMETIMES LIFE DOESN'T ALWAYS GO THE WAY YOU WANT IT TO. SOMETIMES YOU HAVE TO ADAPT TO THE --
wimper

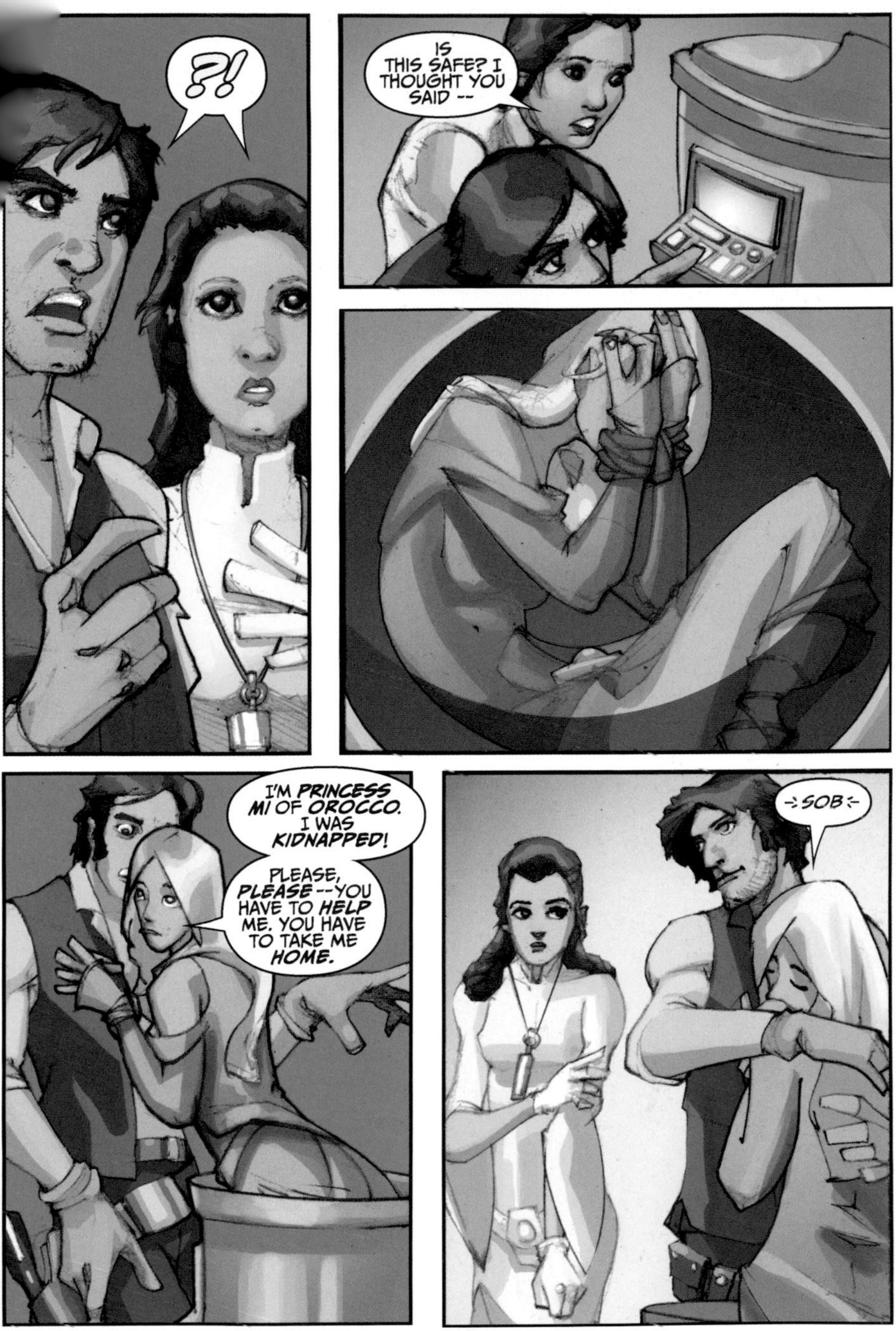
?!
IS THIS SAFE? I THOUGHT YOU SAID --
I'M PRINCESS MI OF OROCCO. I WAS KIDNAPPED!
PLEASE, PLEASE --YOU HAVE TO HELP ME. YOU HAVE TO TAKE ME HOME.
-:-SOB-:-

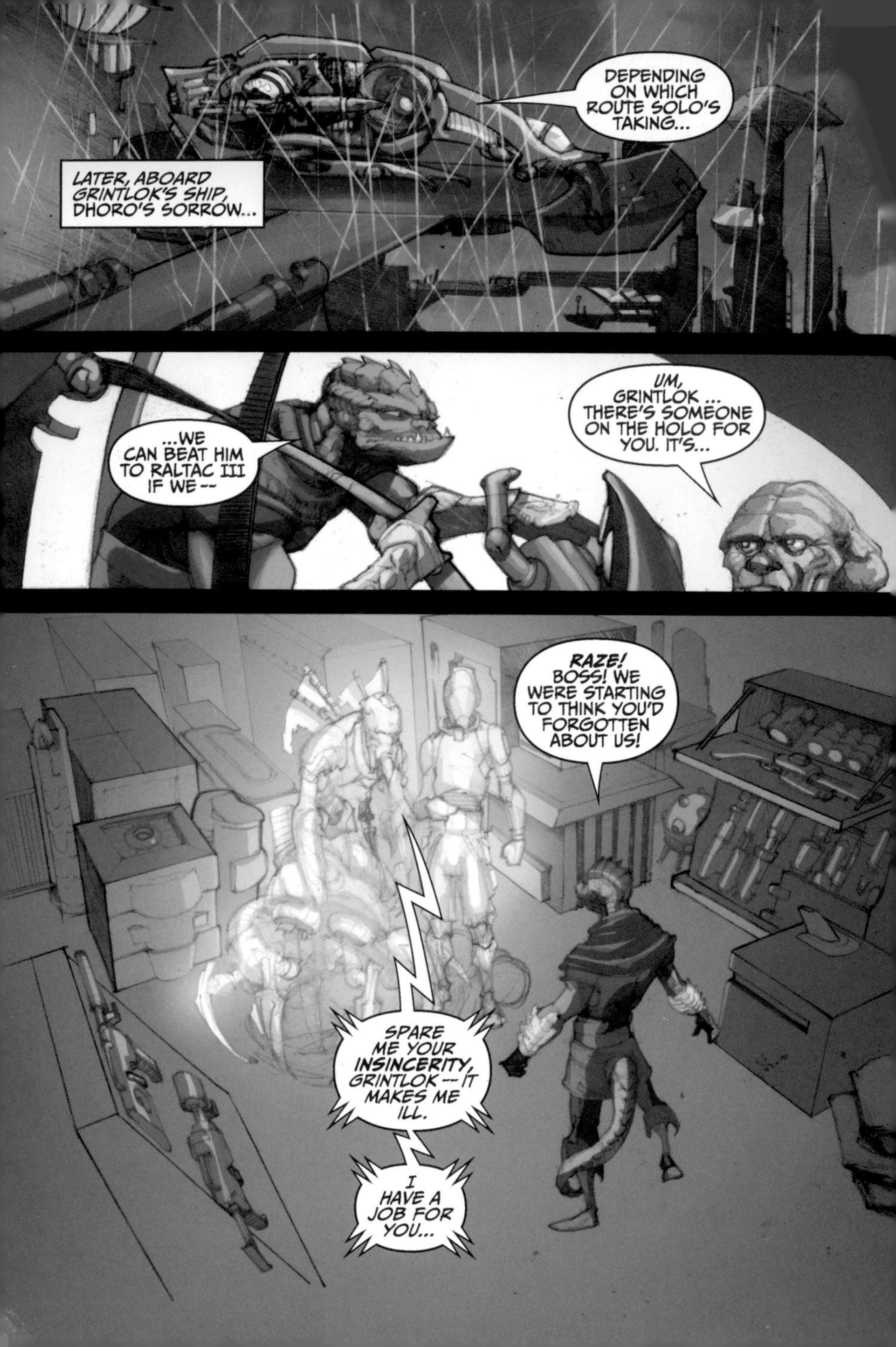
LATER, ABOARD GRINTLOK'S SHIP, DHORO'S SORROW...
DEPENDING ON WHICH ROUTE SOLO'S TAKING...
...WE CAN BEAT HIM TO RALTAC III IF WE --
UM, GRINTLOK ... THERE'S SOMEONE ON THE HOLO FOR YOU. IT'S...
RAZE! BOSS! WE WERE STARTING TO THINK YOU'D FORGOTTEN ABOUT US!
SPARE ME YOUR INSINCERITY, GRINTLOK -- IT MAKES ME ILL.
I HAVE A JOB FOR YOU...

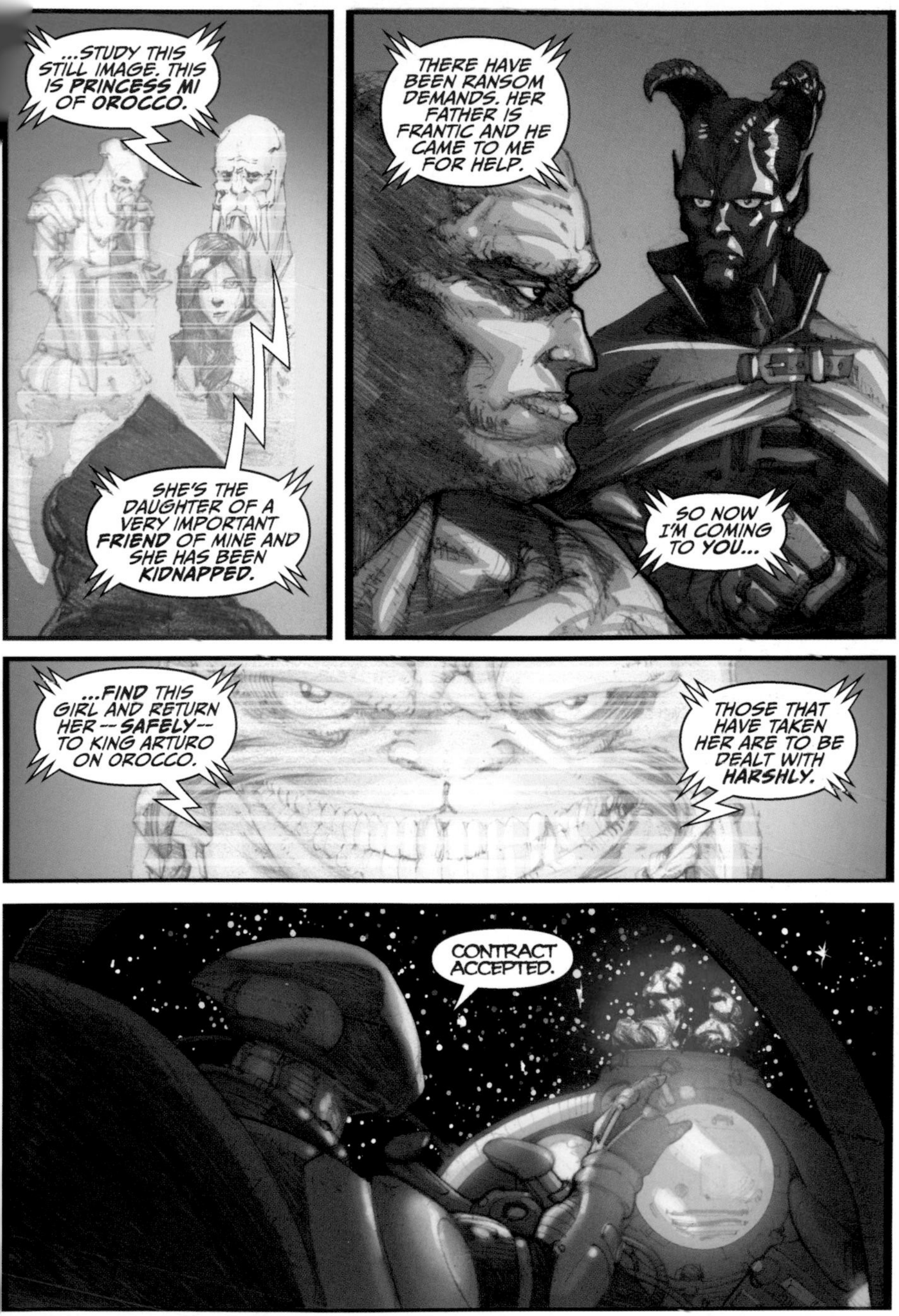
...STUDY THIS STILL IMAGE. THIS IS PRINCESS MI OF OROCCO.
SHE'S THE DAUGHTER OF A VERY IMPORTANT FRIEND OF MINE AND SHE HAS BEEN KIDNAPPED.
THERE HAVE BEEN RANSOM DEMANDS. HER FATHER IS FRANTIC AND HE CAME TO ME FOR HELP.
SO NOW I'M COMING TO YOU...
...FIND THIS GIRL AND RETURN HER -- SAFELY -- TO KING ARTURO ON OROCCO.
THOSE THAT HAVE TAKEN HER ARE TO BE DEALT WITH HARSHLY.
CONTRACT ACCEPTED.

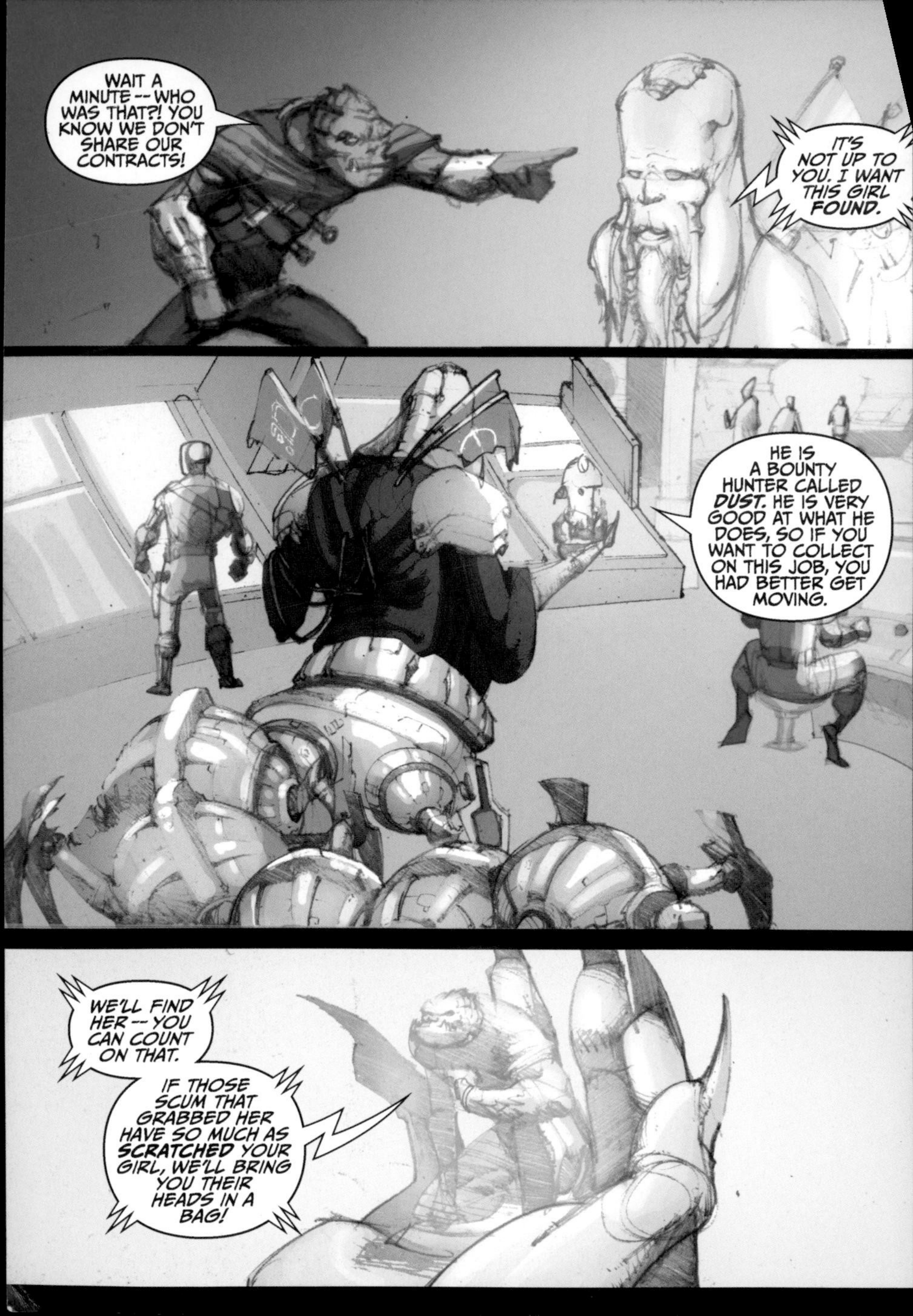
WAIT A MINUTE--WHO WAS THAT?! YOU KNOW WE DON'T SHARE OUR CONTRACTS!
IT'S NOT UP TO YOU. I WANT THIS GIRL **FOUND.**
HE IS A BOUNTY HUNTER CALLED ***DUST.*** HE IS VERY GOOD AT WHAT HE DOES, SO IF YOU WANT TO COLLECT ON THIS JOB, YOU HAD BETTER GET MOVING.
WE'LL FIND HER--YOU CAN COUNT ON THAT.
IF THOSE SCUM THAT GRABBED HER HAVE SO MUCH AS **SCRATCHED** YOUR GIRL, WE'LL BRING YOU THEIR HEADS IN A BAG!

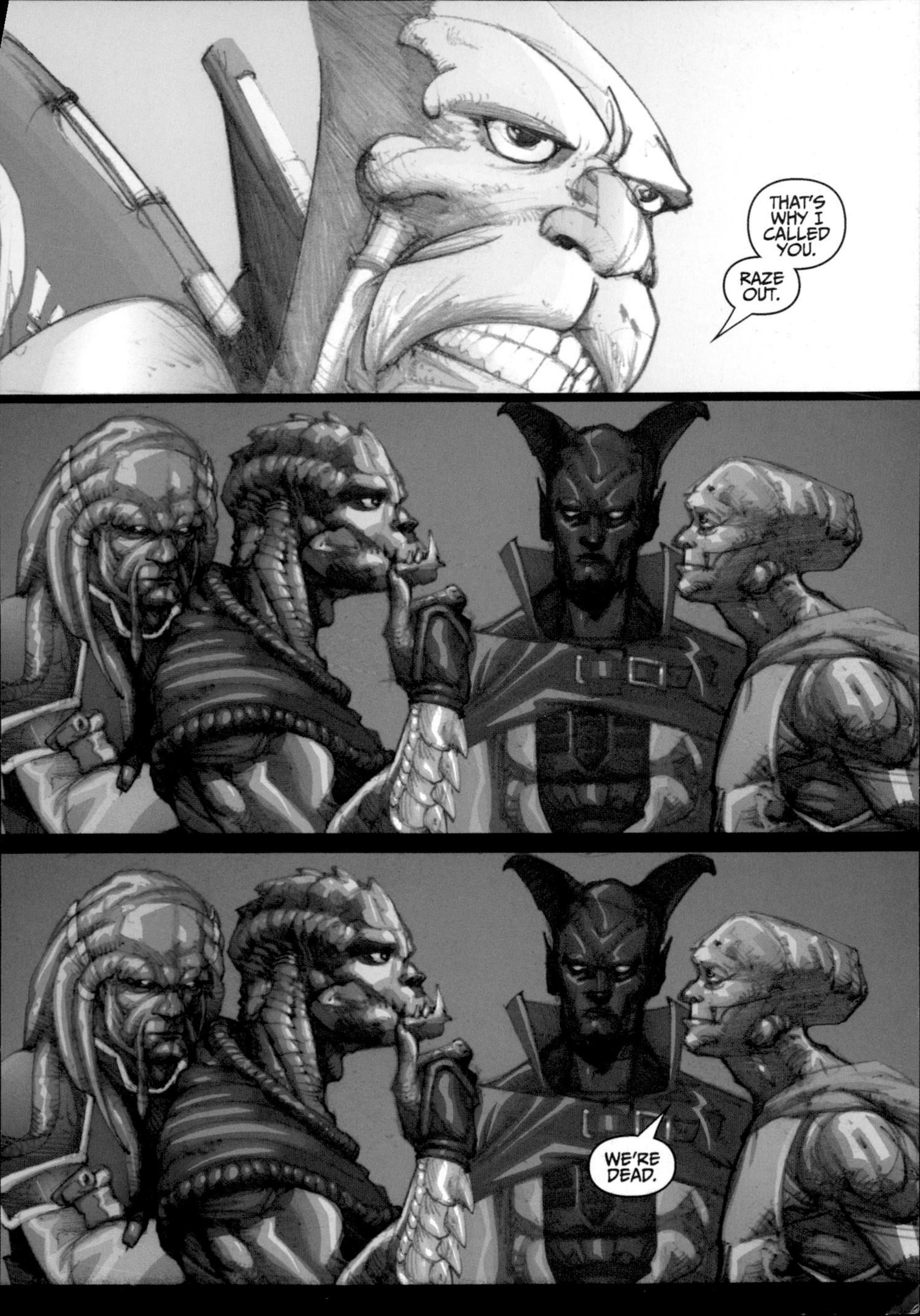
THAT'S WHY I CALLED YOU.
RAZE OUT.
WE'RE DEAD.

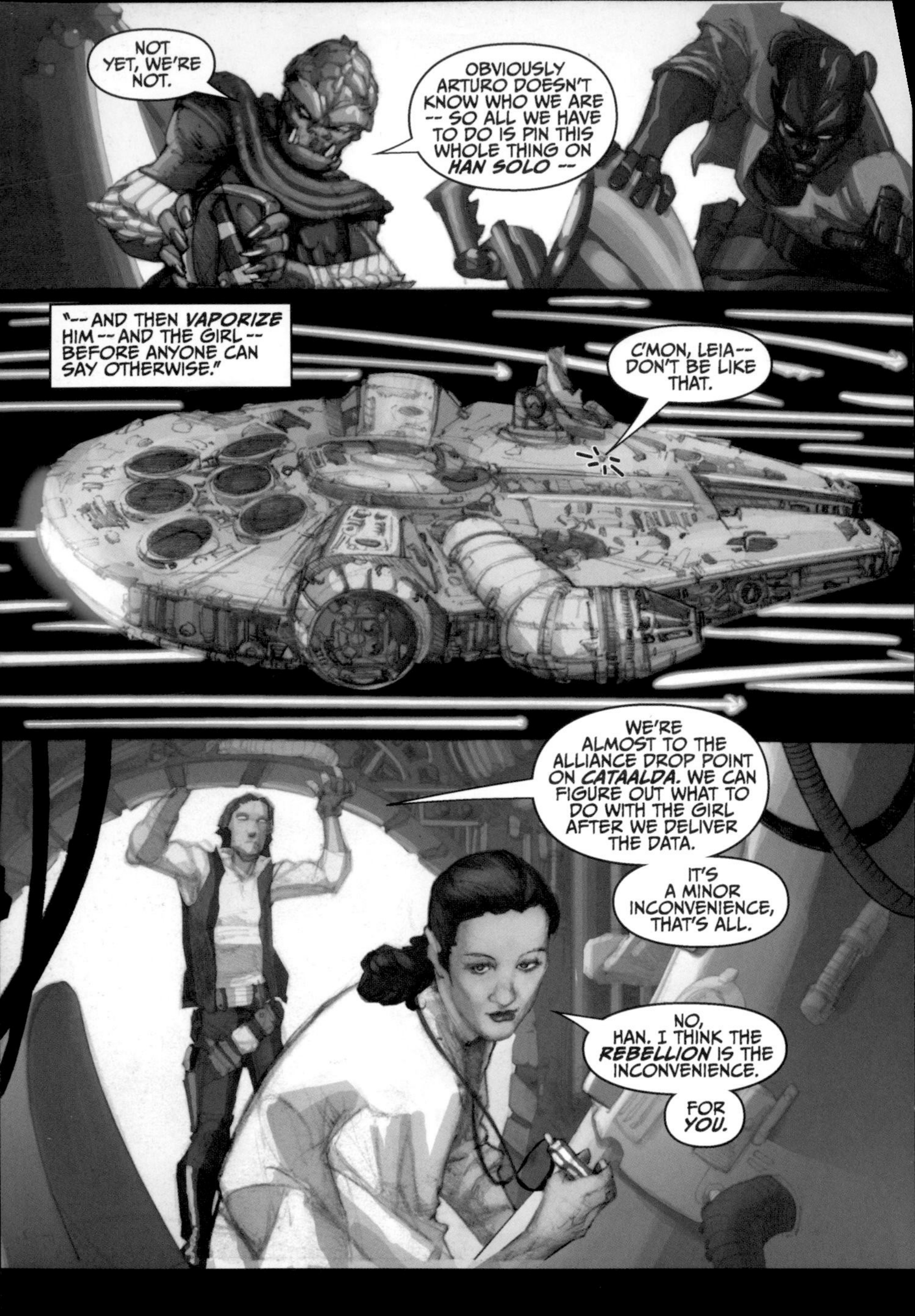
NOT YET, WE'RE NOT.
OBVIOUSLY ARTURO DOESN'T KNOW WHO WE ARE -- SO ALL WE HAVE TO DO IS PIN THIS WHOLE THING ON HAN SOLO --
"-- AND THEN VAPORIZE HIM -- AND THE GIRL -- BEFORE ANYONE CAN SAY OTHERWISE."
C'MON, LEIA-- DON'T BE LIKE THAT.
WE'RE ALMOST TO THE ALLIANCE DROP POINT ON CATAALDA. WE CAN FIGURE OUT WHAT TO DO WITH THE GIRL AFTER WE DELIVER THE DATA.
IT'S A MINOR INCONVENIENCE, THAT'S ALL.
NO, HAN. I THINK THE REBELLION IS THE INCONVENIENCE.
FOR YOU.

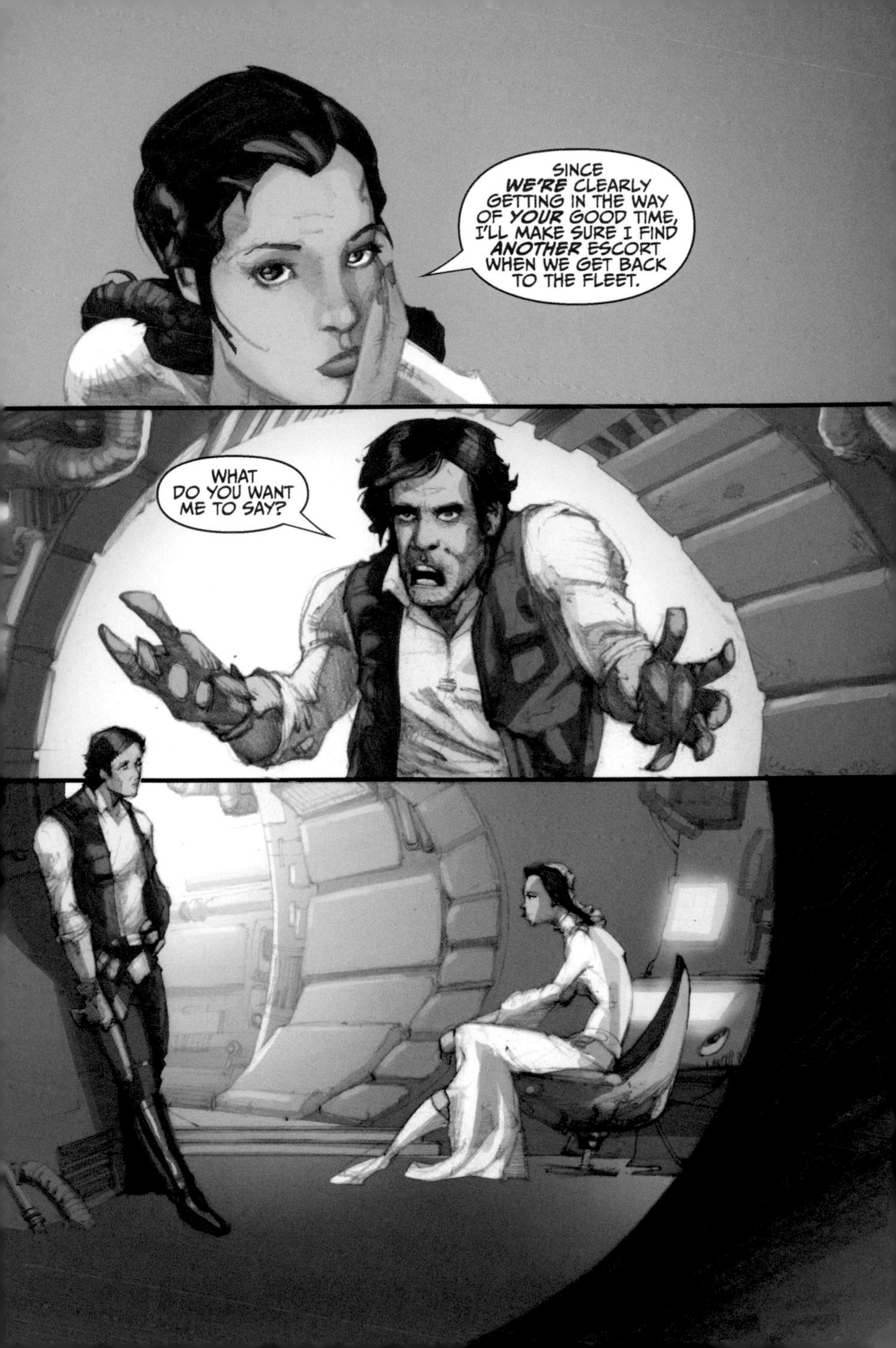
SINCE *WE'RE* CLEARLY GETTING IN THE WAY OF *YOUR* GOOD TIME, I'LL MAKE SURE I FIND *ANOTHER* ESCORT WHEN WE GET BACK TO THE FLEET.
WHAT DO YOU WANT ME TO SAY?

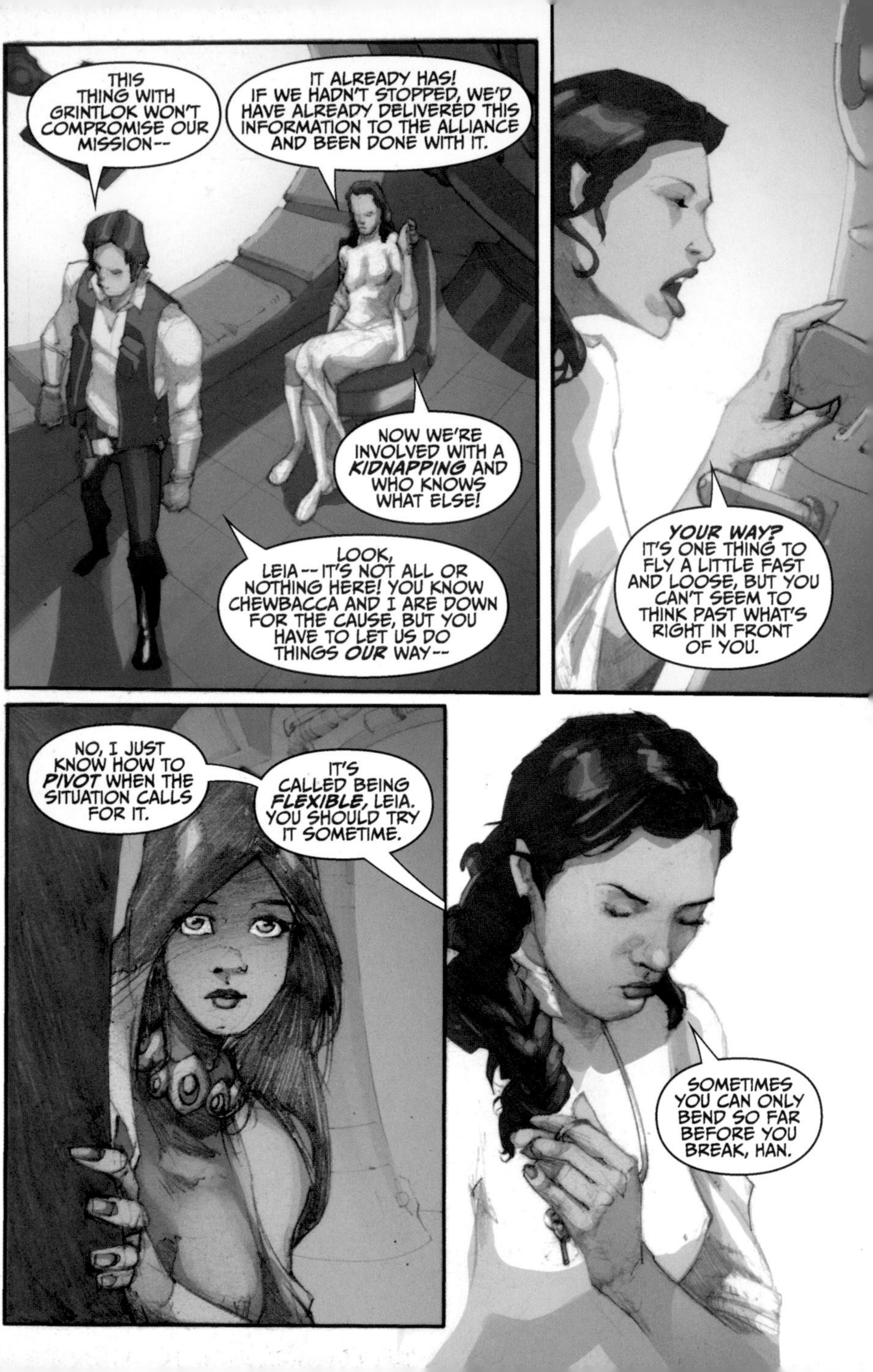
THIS THING WITH GRINTLOK WON'T COMPROMISE OUR MISSION--
IT ALREADY HAS! IF WE HADN'T STOPPED, WE'D HAVE ALREADY DELIVERED THIS INFORMATION TO THE ALLIANCE AND BEEN DONE WITH IT.
NOW WE'RE INVOLVED WITH A *KIDNAPPING* AND WHO KNOWS WHAT ELSE!
LOOK, LEIA-- IT'S NOT ALL OR NOTHING HERE! YOU KNOW CHEWBACCA AND I ARE DOWN FOR THE CAUSE, BUT YOU HAVE TO LET US DO THINGS *OUR* WAY--
YOUR WAY? IT'S ONE THING TO FLY A LITTLE FAST AND LOOSE, BUT YOU CAN'T SEEM TO THINK PAST WHAT'S RIGHT IN FRONT OF YOU.
NO, I JUST KNOW HOW TO *PIVOT* WHEN THE SITUATION CALLS FOR IT.
IT'S CALLED BEING *FLEXIBLE,* LEIA. YOU SHOULD TRY IT SOMETIME.
SOMETIMES YOU CAN ONLY BEND SO FAR BEFORE YOU BREAK, HAN.

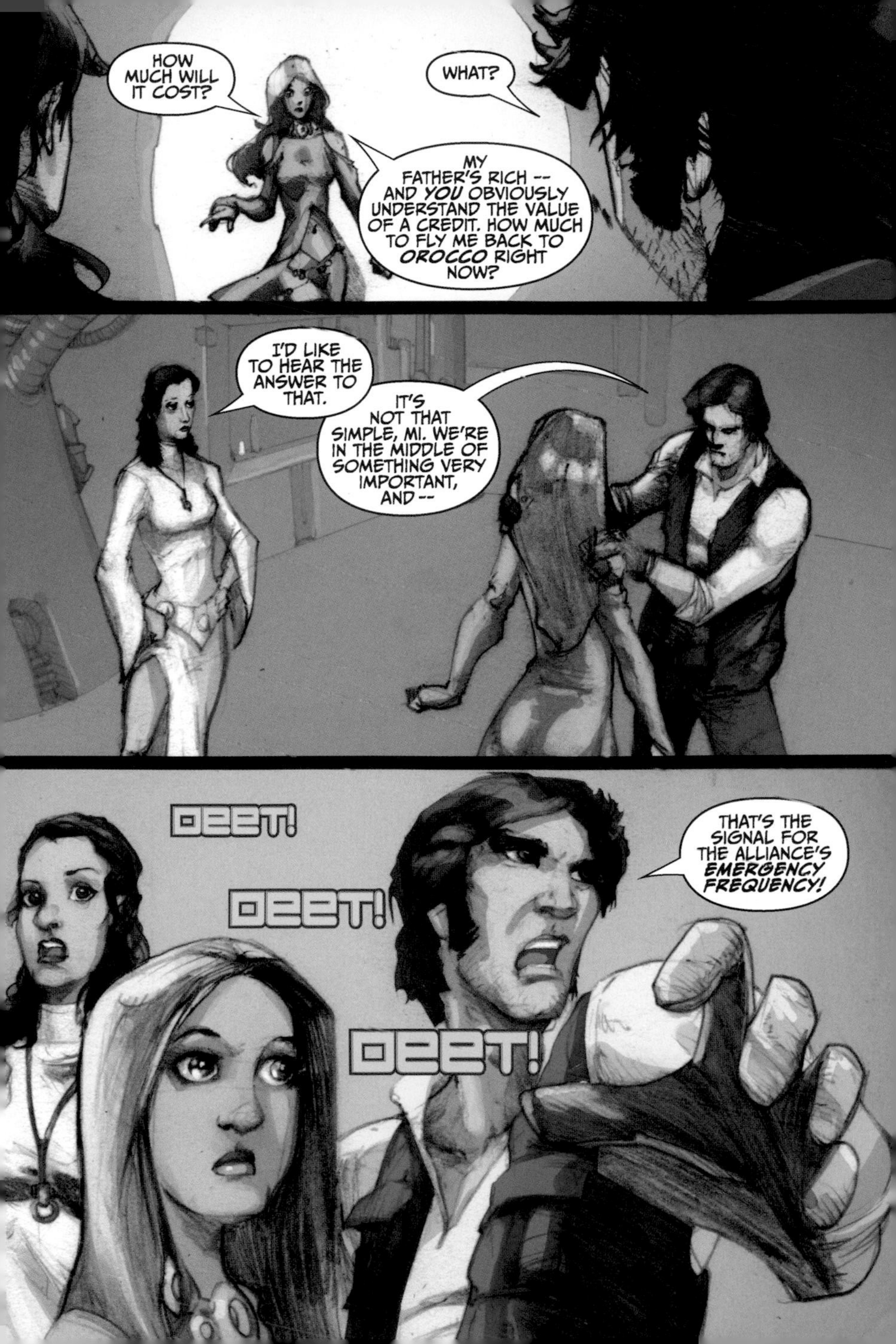
HOW MUCH WILL IT COST?
WHAT?
MY FATHER'S RICH -- AND *YOU* OBVIOUSLY UNDERSTAND THE VALUE OF A CREDIT. HOW MUCH TO FLY ME BACK TO *OROCCO* RIGHT NOW?
I'D LIKE TO HEAR THE ANSWER TO THAT.
IT'S NOT THAT SIMPLE, MI. WE'RE IN THE MIDDLE OF SOMETHING VERY IMPORTANT, AND --
DEET!
DEET!
DEET!
THAT'S THE SIGNAL FOR THE ALLIANCE'S *EMERGENCY FREQUENCY!*

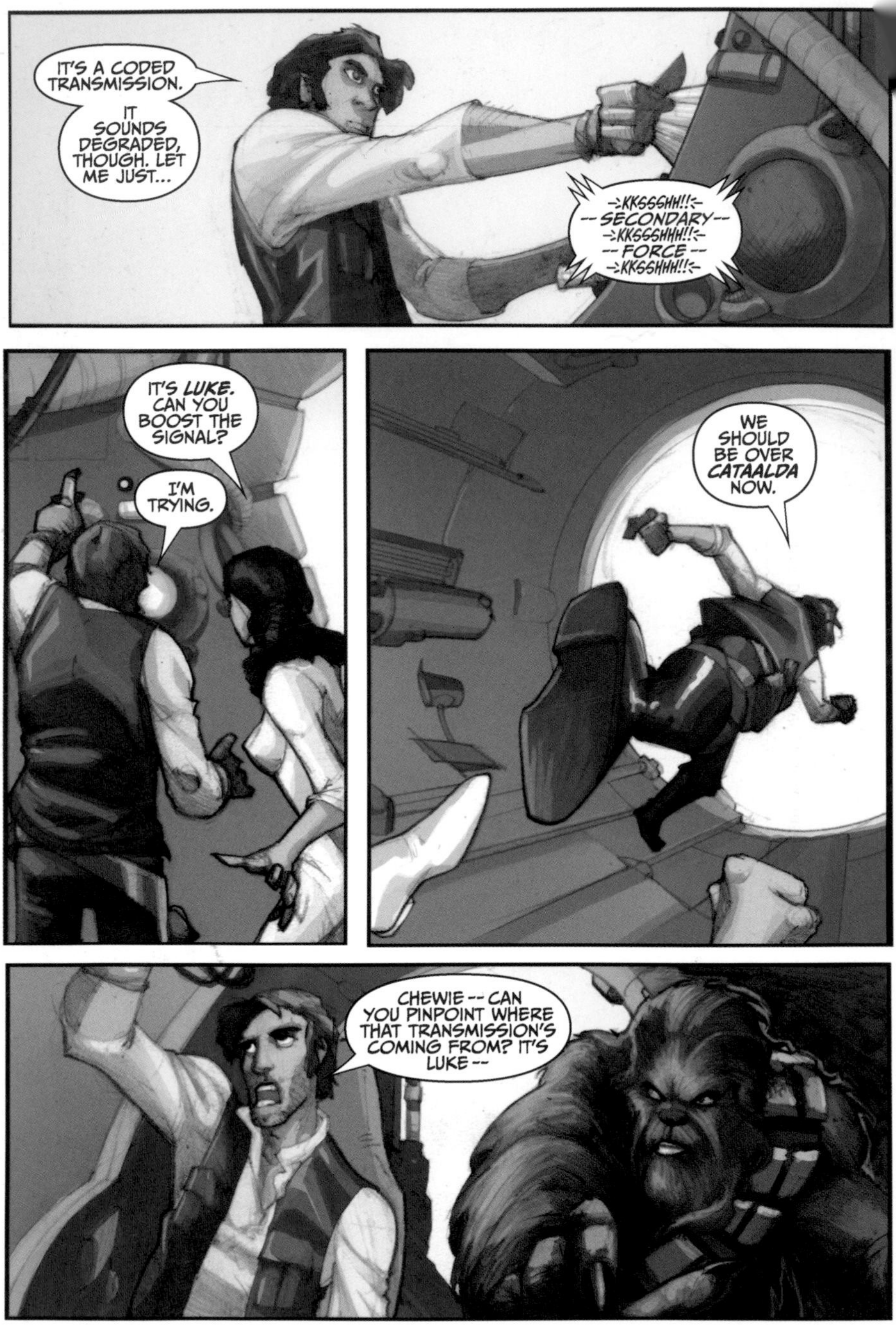
IT'S A CODED TRANSMISSION.
IT SOUNDS DEGRADED, THOUGH. LET ME JUST...
-KKSSSHH!!- --SECONDARY-- -KKSSSHHH!!- --FORCE-- -KKSSHHH!!-
IT'S LUKE. CAN YOU BOOST THE SIGNAL?
I'M TRYING.
WE SHOULD BE OVER CATAALDA NOW.
CHEWIE -- CAN YOU PINPOINT WHERE THAT TRANSMISSION'S COMING FROM? IT'S LUKE --

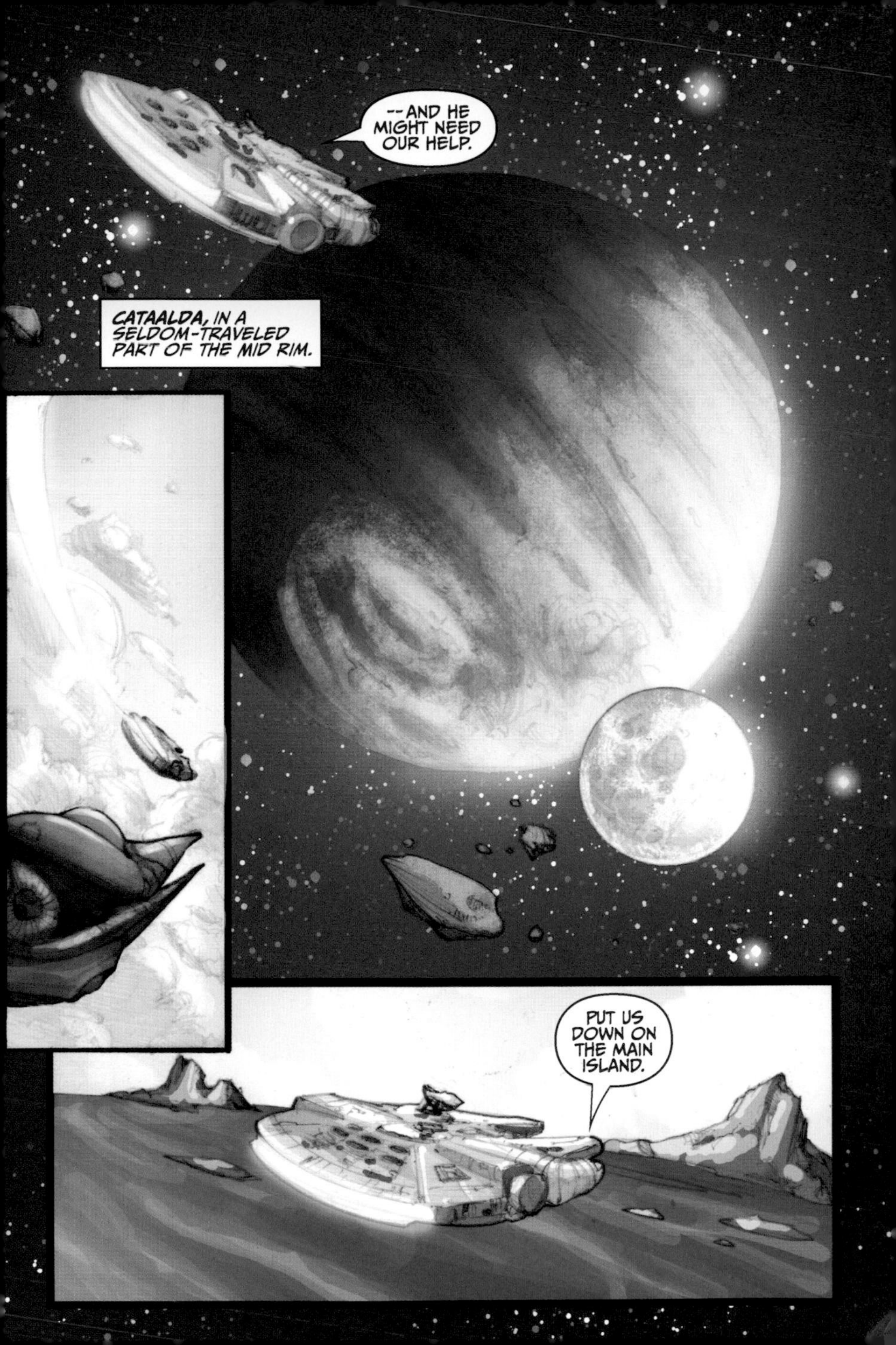
--AND HE MIGHT NEED OUR HELP.
CATAALDA, IN A SELDOM-TRAVELED PART OF THE MID RIM.
PUT US DOWN ON THE MAIN ISLAND.

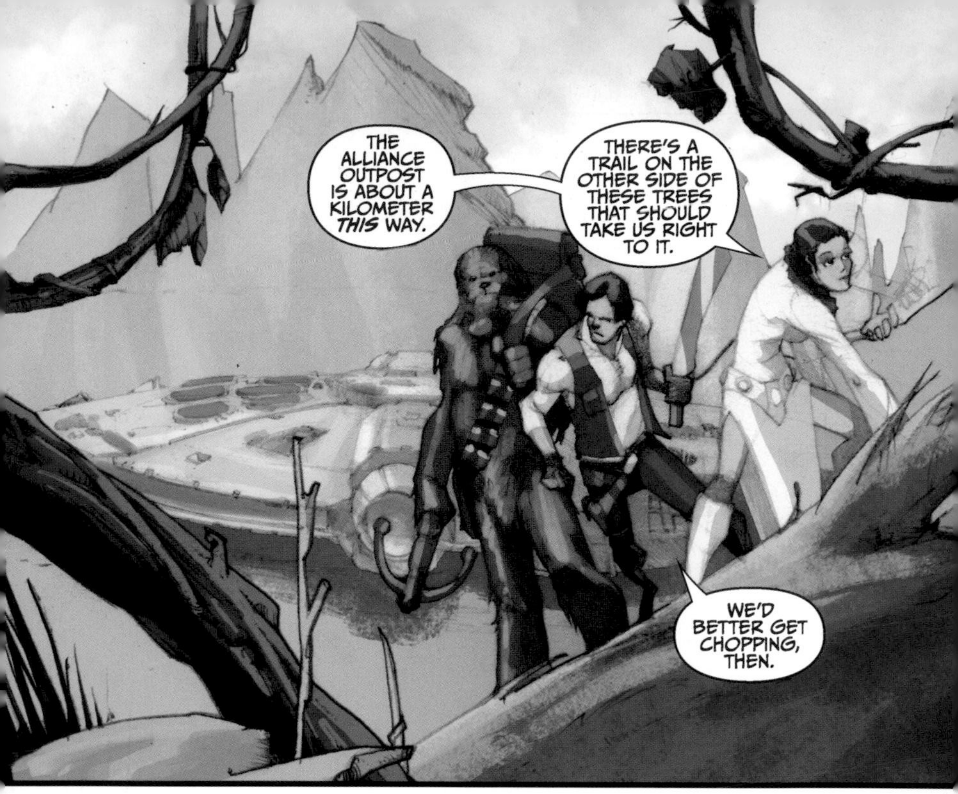
THE ALLIANCE OUTPOST IS ABOUT A KILOMETER *THIS* WAY.
THERE'S A TRAIL ON THE OTHER SIDE OF THESE TREES THAT SHOULD TAKE US RIGHT TO IT.
WE'D BETTER GET CHOPPING, THEN.

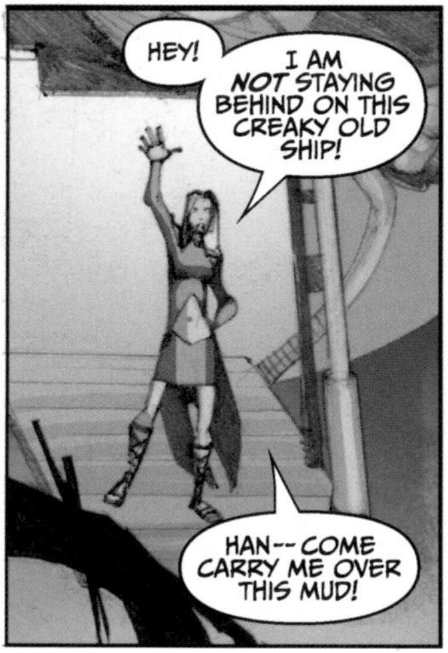
HEY!
I AM *NOT* STAYING BEHIND ON THIS CREAKY OLD SHIP!
HAN-- COME CARRY ME OVER THIS MUD!

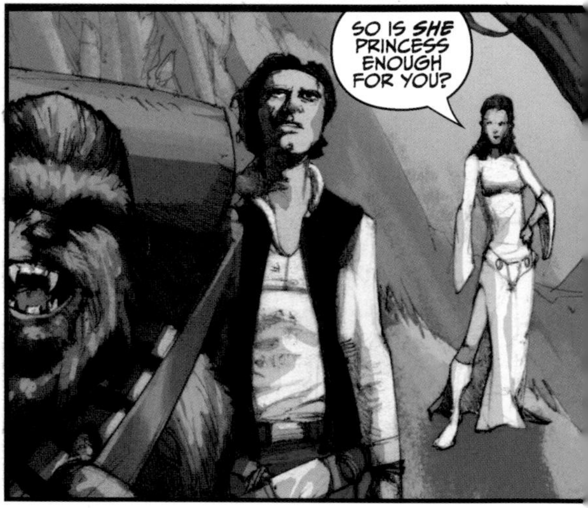
SO IS *SHE* PRINCESS ENOUGH FOR YOU?

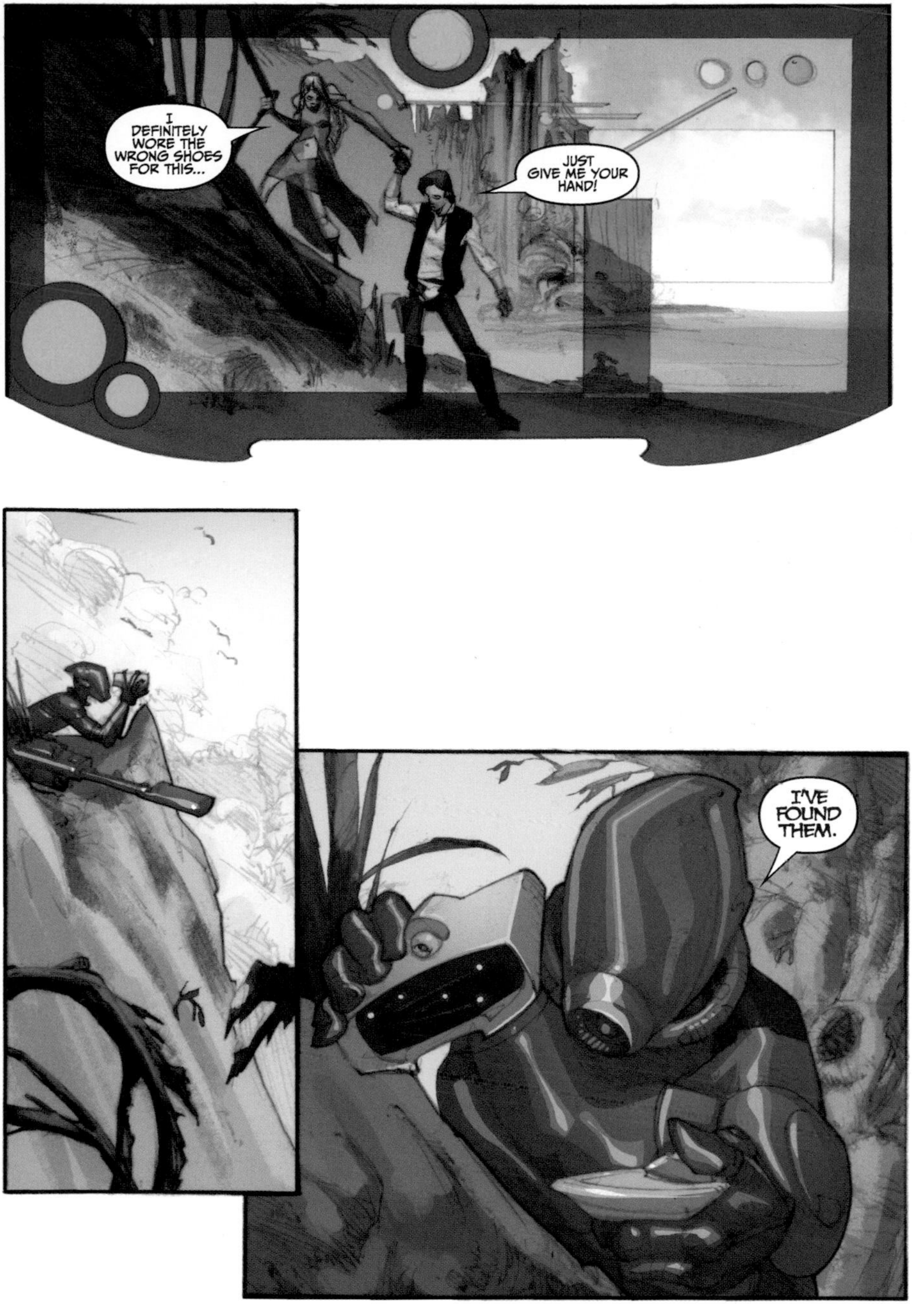
I DEFINITELY WORE THE WRONG SHOES FOR THIS...
JUST GIVE ME YOUR HAND!
I'VE FOUND THEM.

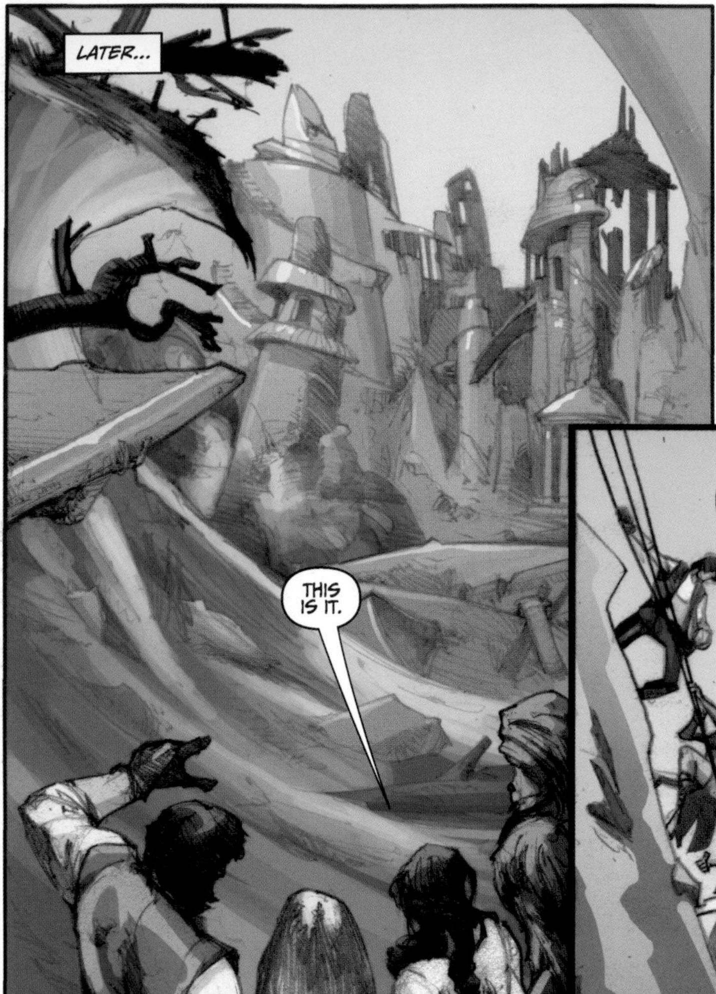
LATER...
THIS IS IT.

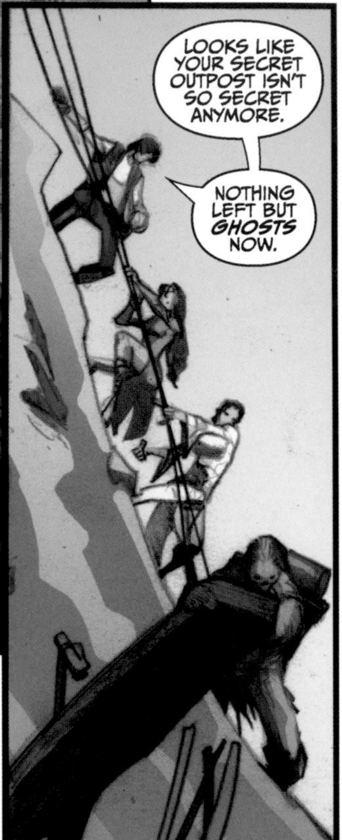
LOOKS LIKE YOUR SECRET OUTPOST ISN'T SO SECRET ANYMORE.
NOTHING LEFT BUT GHOSTS NOW.

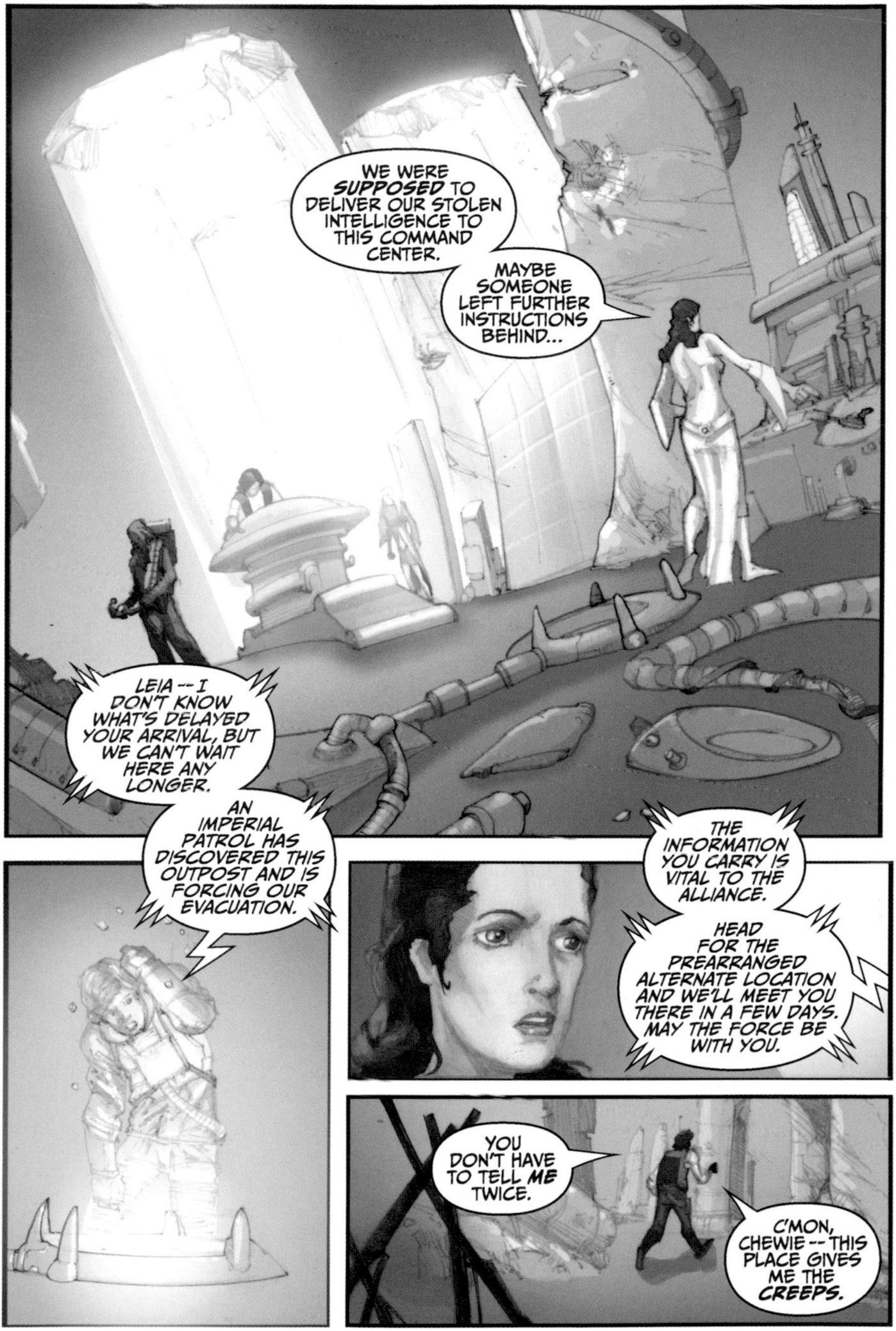
WE WERE SUPPOSED TO DELIVER OUR STOLEN INTELLIGENCE TO THIS COMMAND CENTER.
MAYBE SOMEONE LEFT FURTHER INSTRUCTIONS BEHIND...
LEIA -- I DON'T KNOW WHAT'S DELAYED YOUR ARRIVAL, BUT WE CAN'T WAIT HERE ANY LONGER.
AN IMPERIAL PATROL HAS DISCOVERED THIS OUTPOST AND IS FORCING OUR EVACUATION.
THE INFORMATION YOU CARRY IS VITAL TO THE ALLIANCE.
HEAD FOR THE PREARRANGED ALTERNATE LOCATION AND WE'LL MEET YOU THERE IN A FEW DAYS. MAY THE FORCE BE WITH YOU.
YOU DON'T HAVE TO TELL ME TWICE.
C'MON, CHEWIE -- THIS PLACE GIVES ME THE CREEPS.

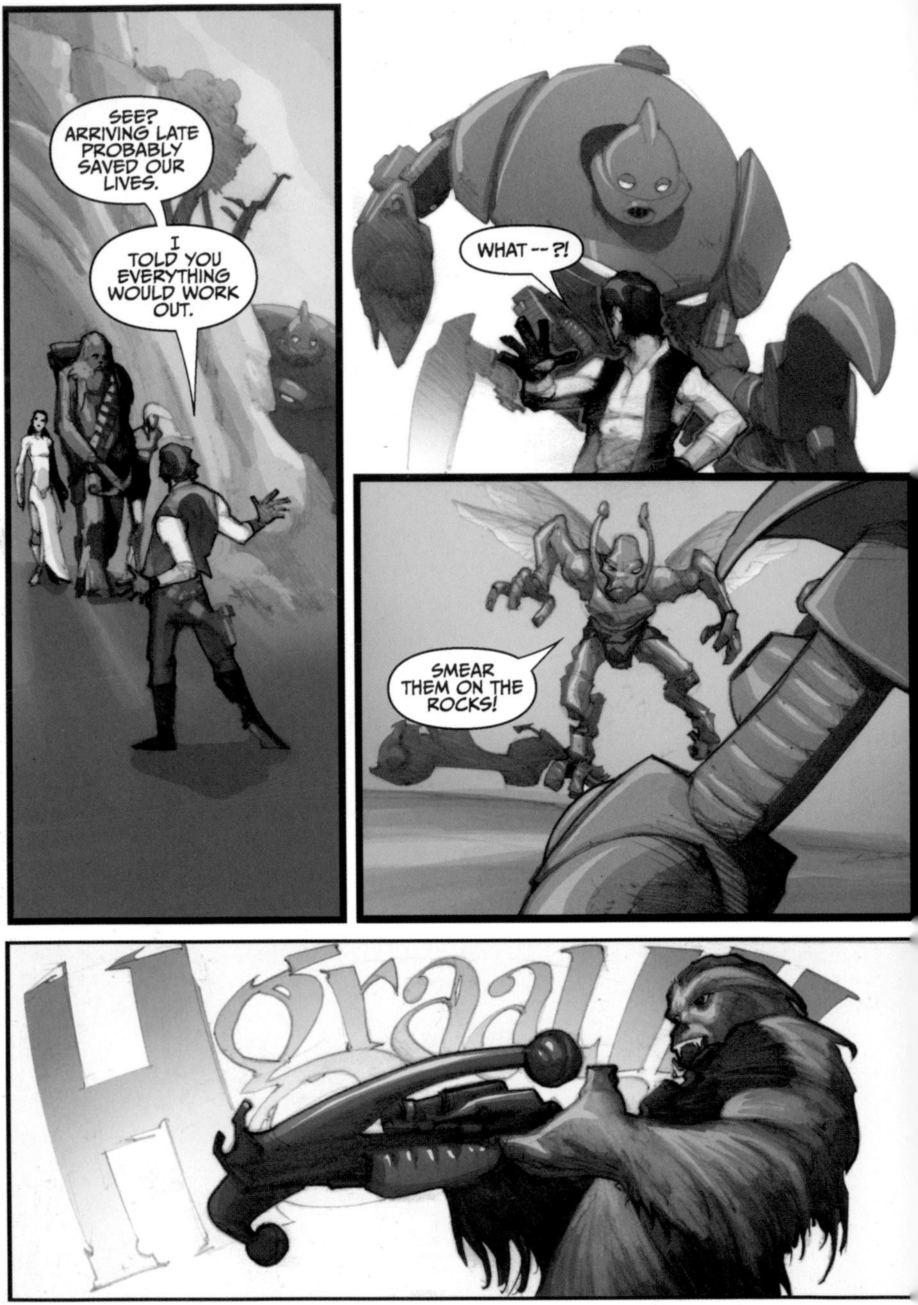
SEE? ARRIVING LATE PROBABLY SAVED OUR LIVES.
I TOLD YOU EVERYTHING WOULD WORK OUT.
WHAT --?!
SMEAR THEM ON THE ROCKS!

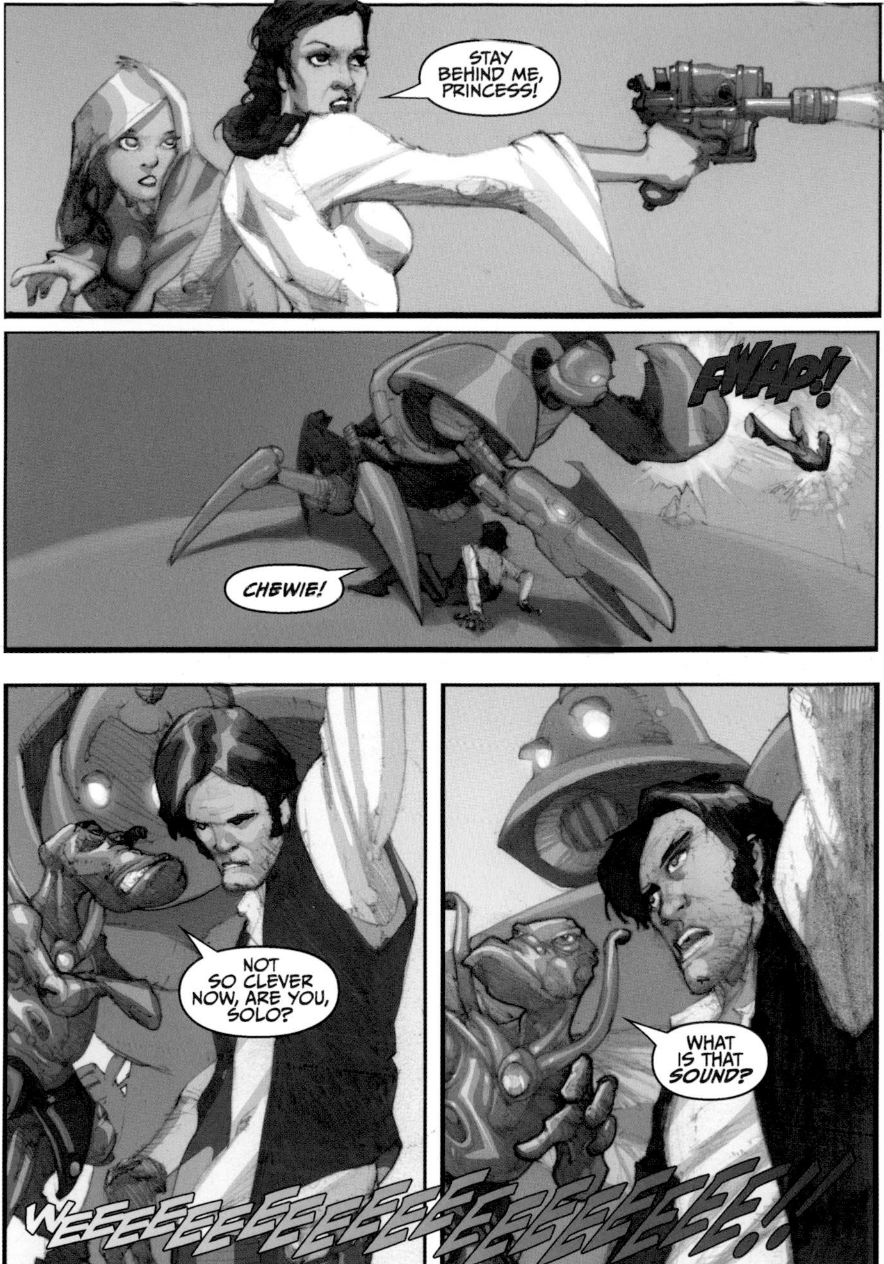
STAY BEHIND ME, PRINCESS!
FWAP!!
CHEWIE!
NOT SO CLEVER NOW, ARE YOU, SOLO?
WHAT IS THAT SOUND?
WEEEEEEEEEEEEEEEEEEEEEEEEEEE!!

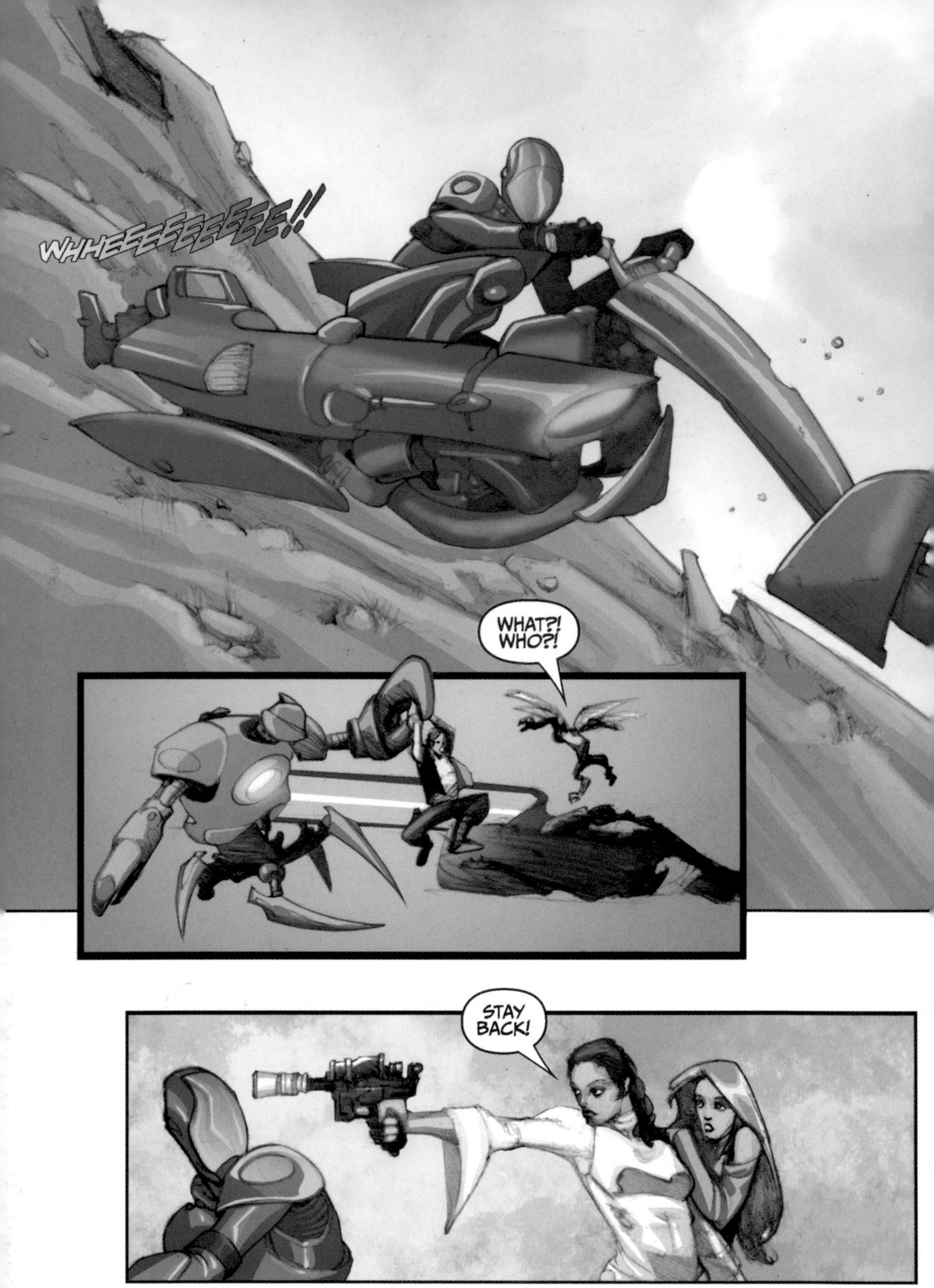
WHHEEEEEEEEEEEE!!
WHAT?! WHO?!
STAY BACK!

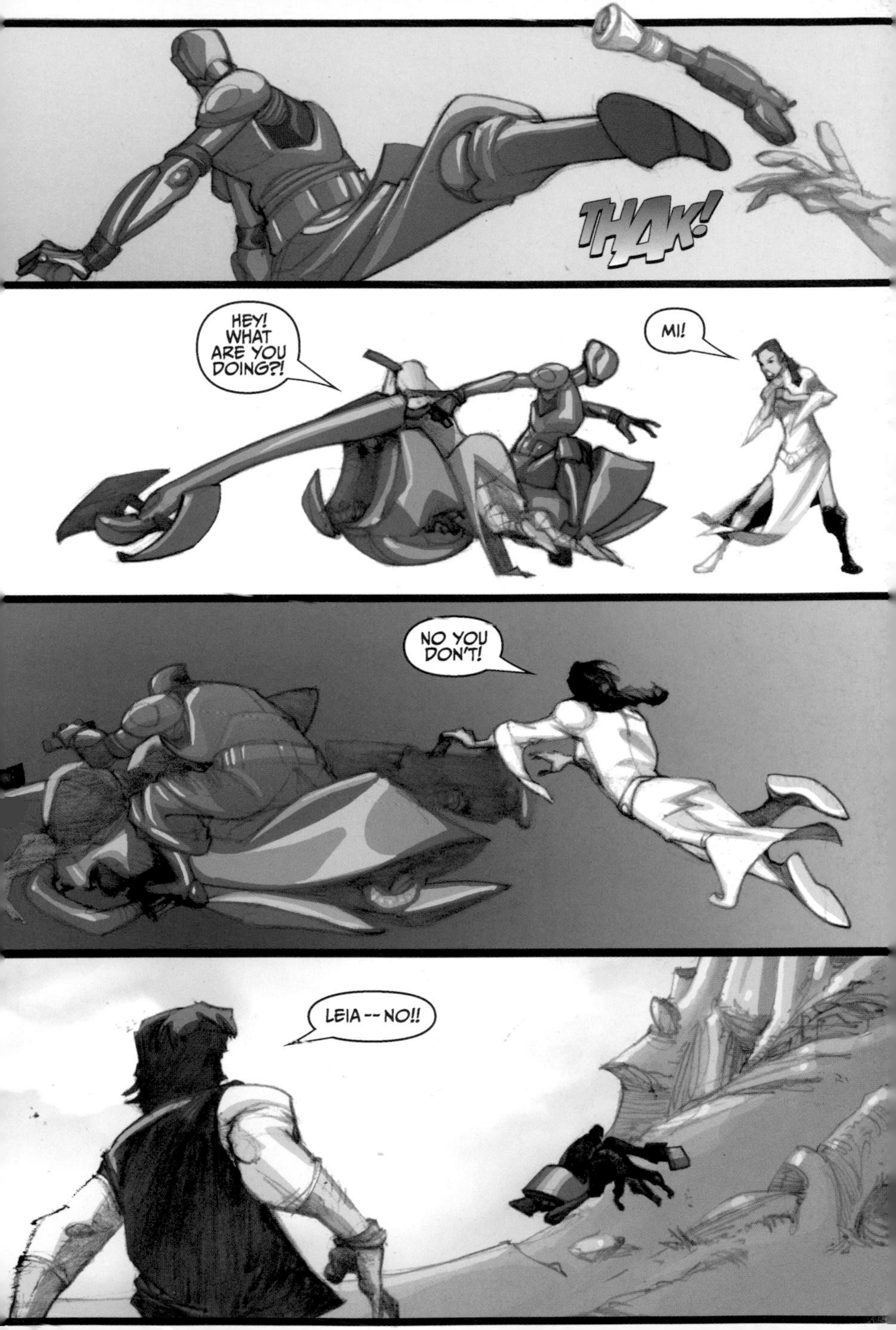
THAK!
HEY! WHAT ARE YOU DOING?!
MI!
NO YOU DON'T!
LEIA--NO!!

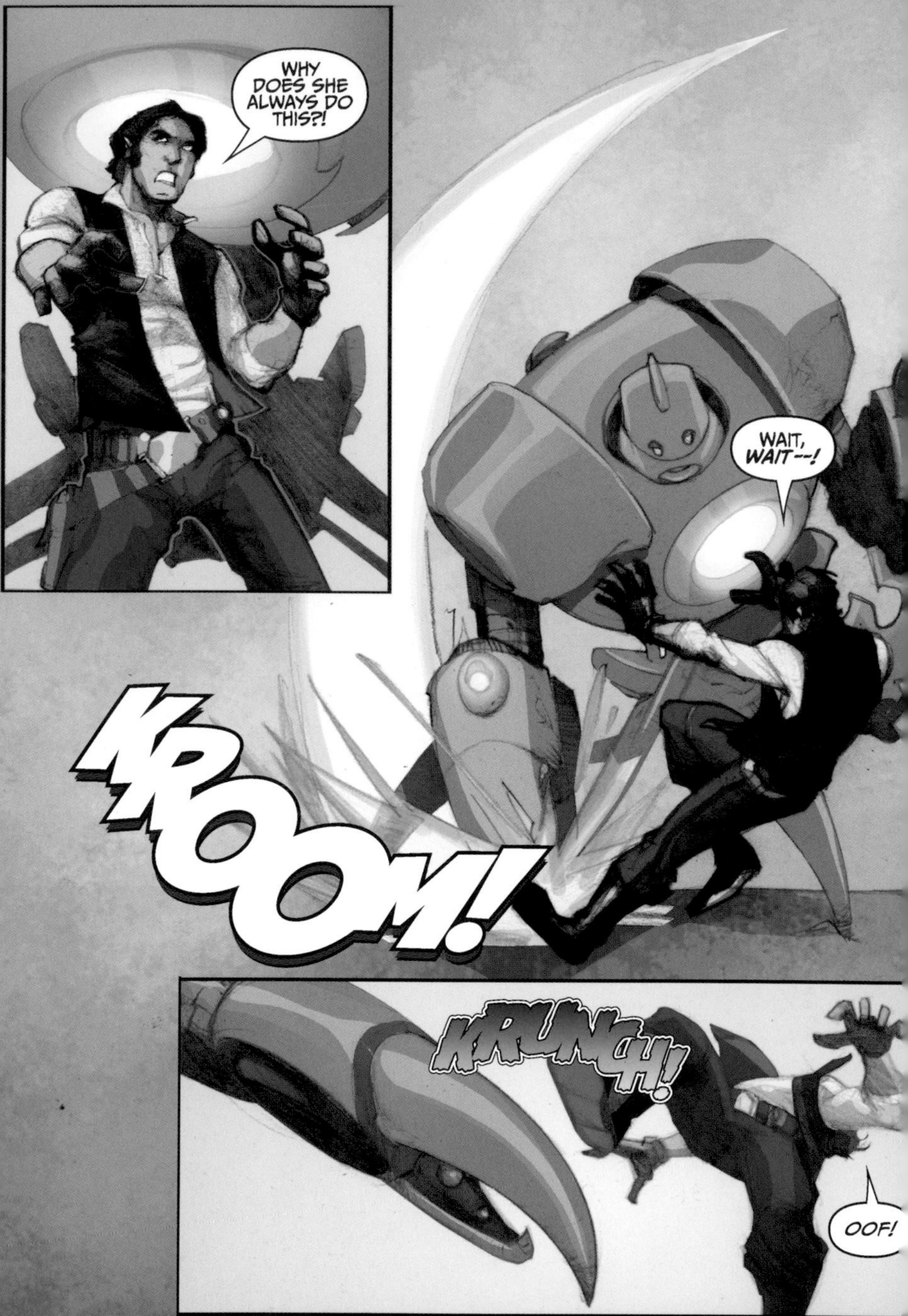

WHY DOES SHE ALWAYS DO THIS?!
WAIT, WAIT--!
KROOM!
KRUNCH!
OOF!

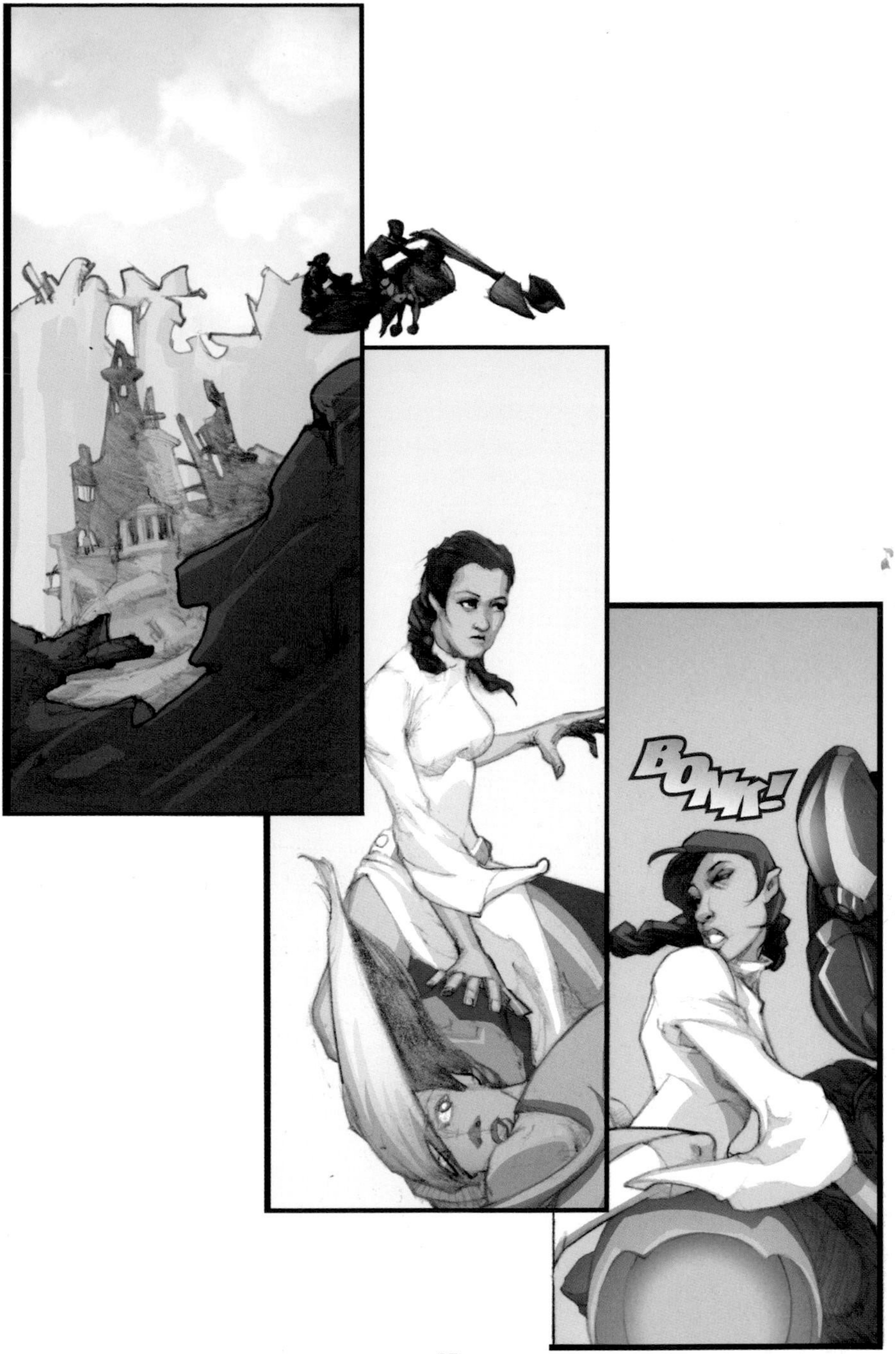
BONK!

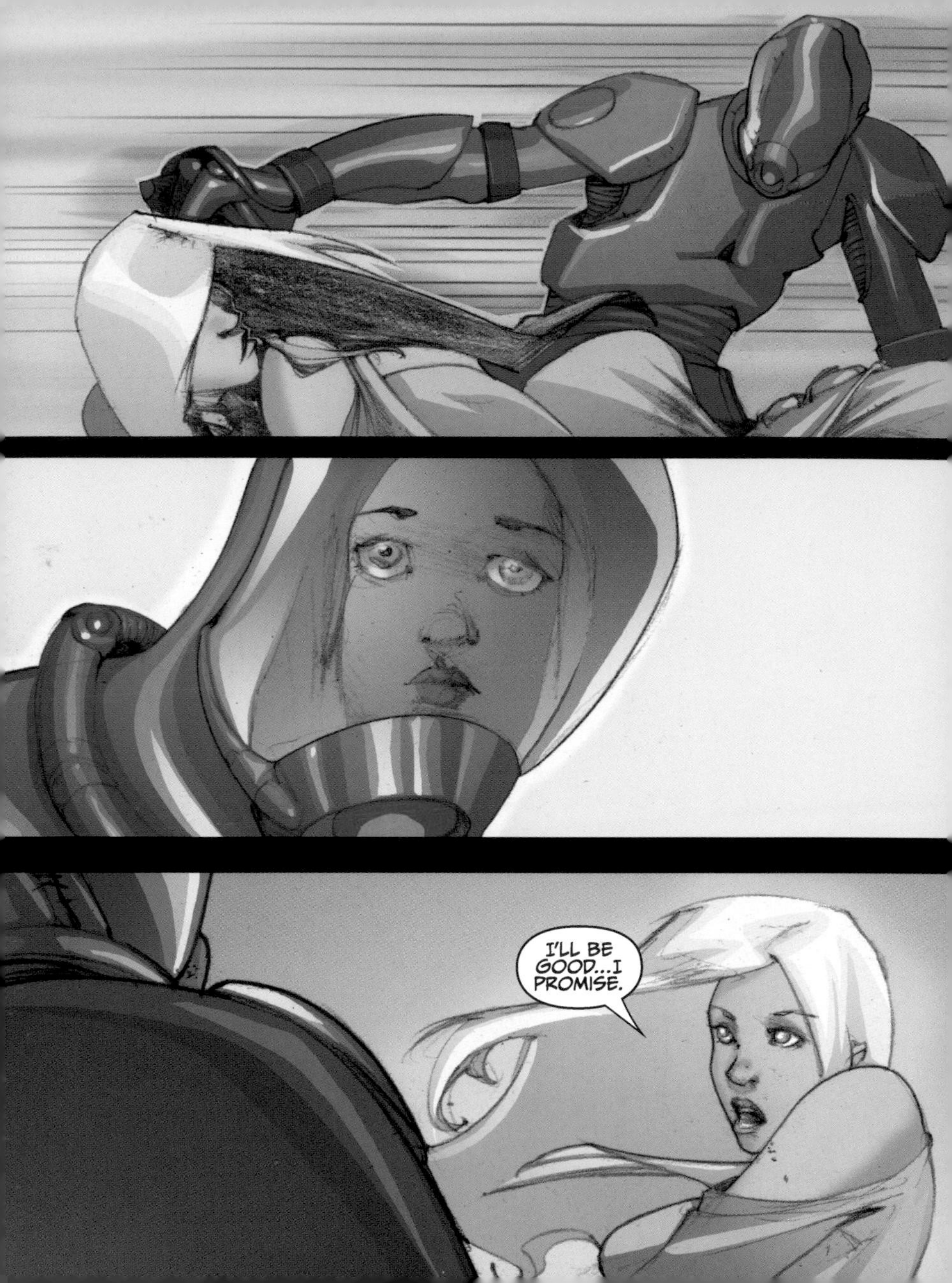
I'LL BE GOOD...I PROMISE.

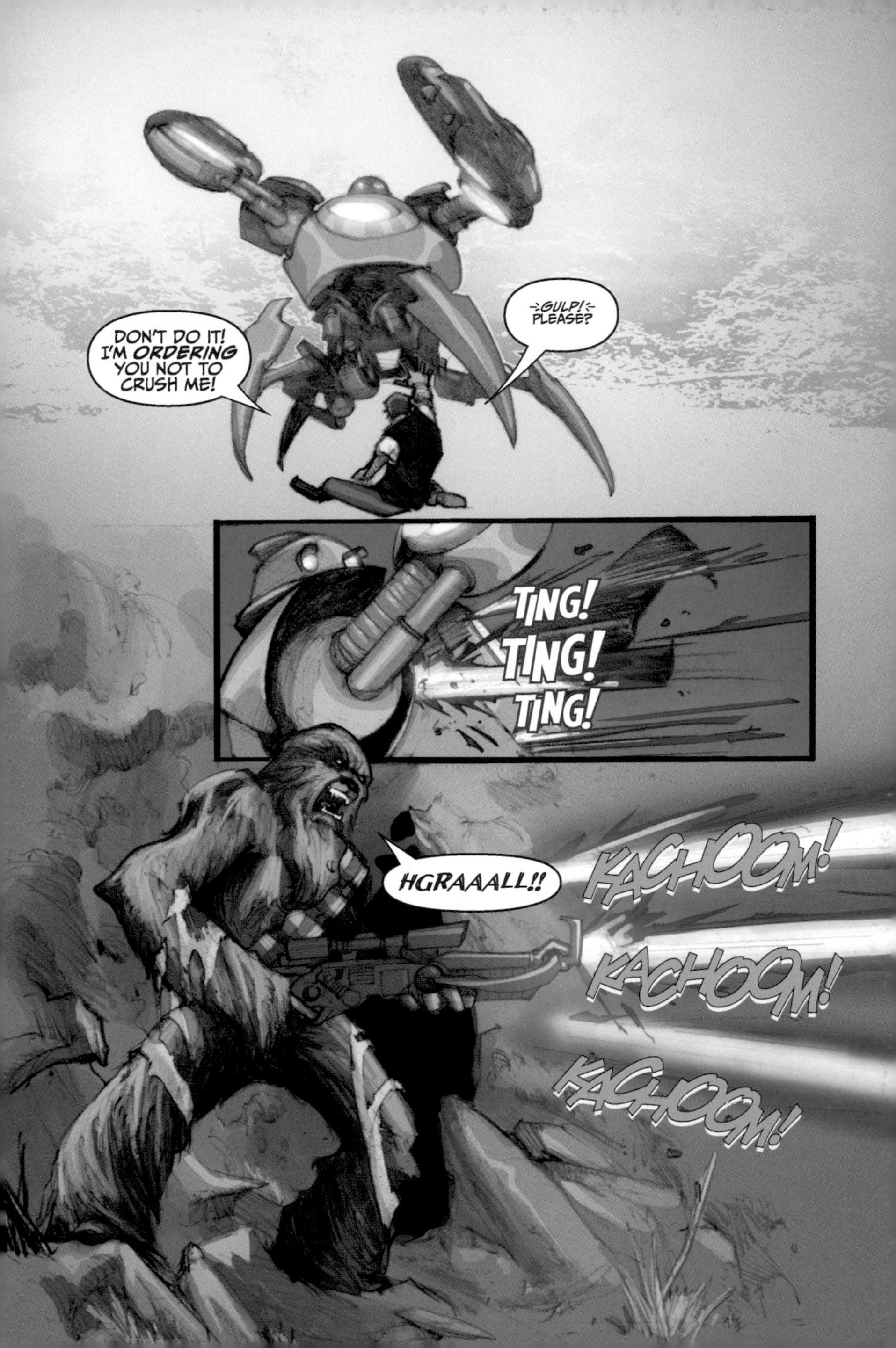
DON'T DO IT! I'M ORDERING YOU NOT TO CRUSH ME!
-GULP!- PLEASE?
TING! TING! TING!
HGRAAALL!!
KACHOOM! KACHOOM! KACHOOM!

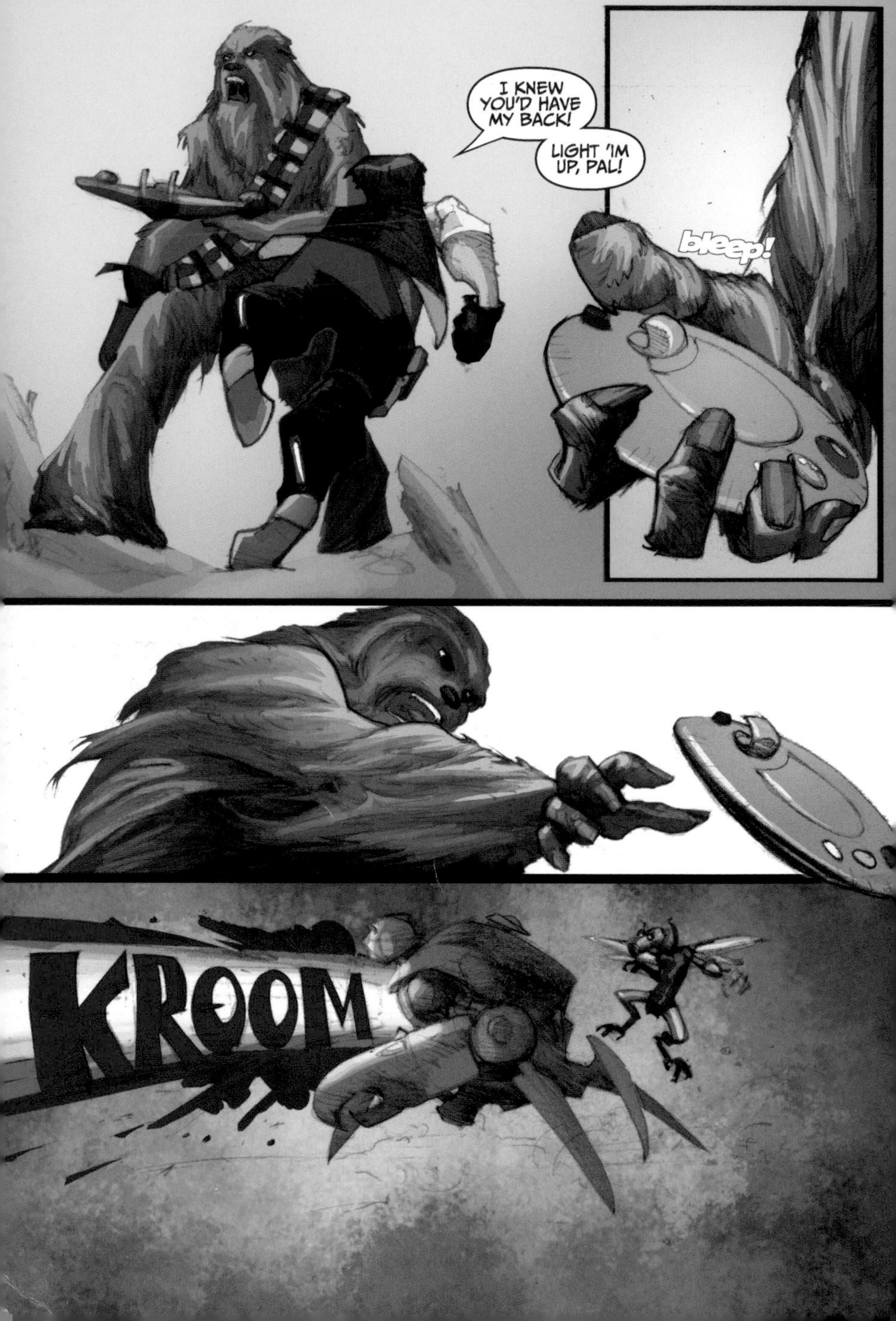
I KNEW YOU'D HAVE MY BACK!
LIGHT 'IM UP, PAL!
bleep!
KROOM

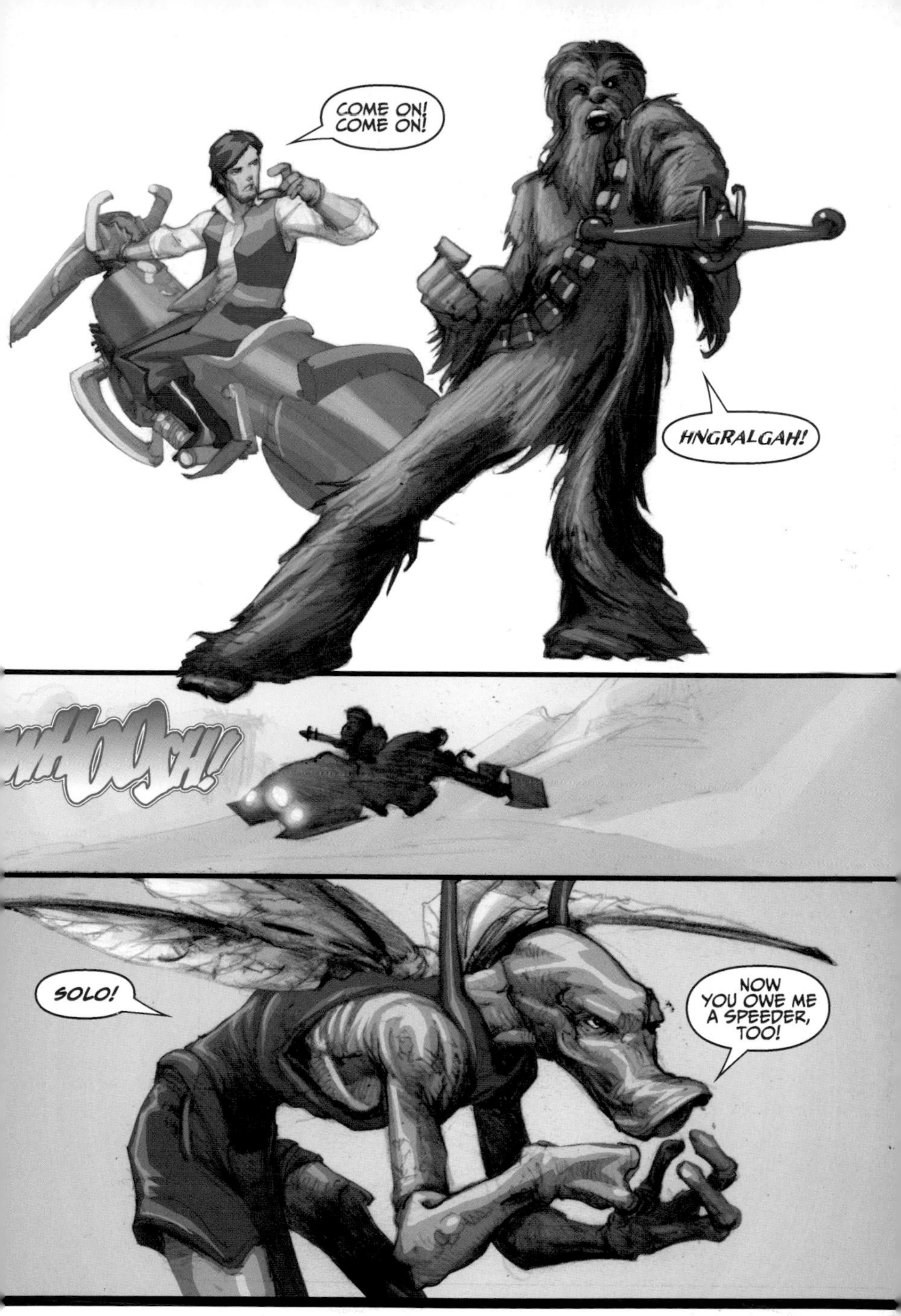
COME ON! COME ON!
HNGRALGAH!
WHOOSH!
SOLO!
NOW YOU OWE ME A SPEEDER, TOO!

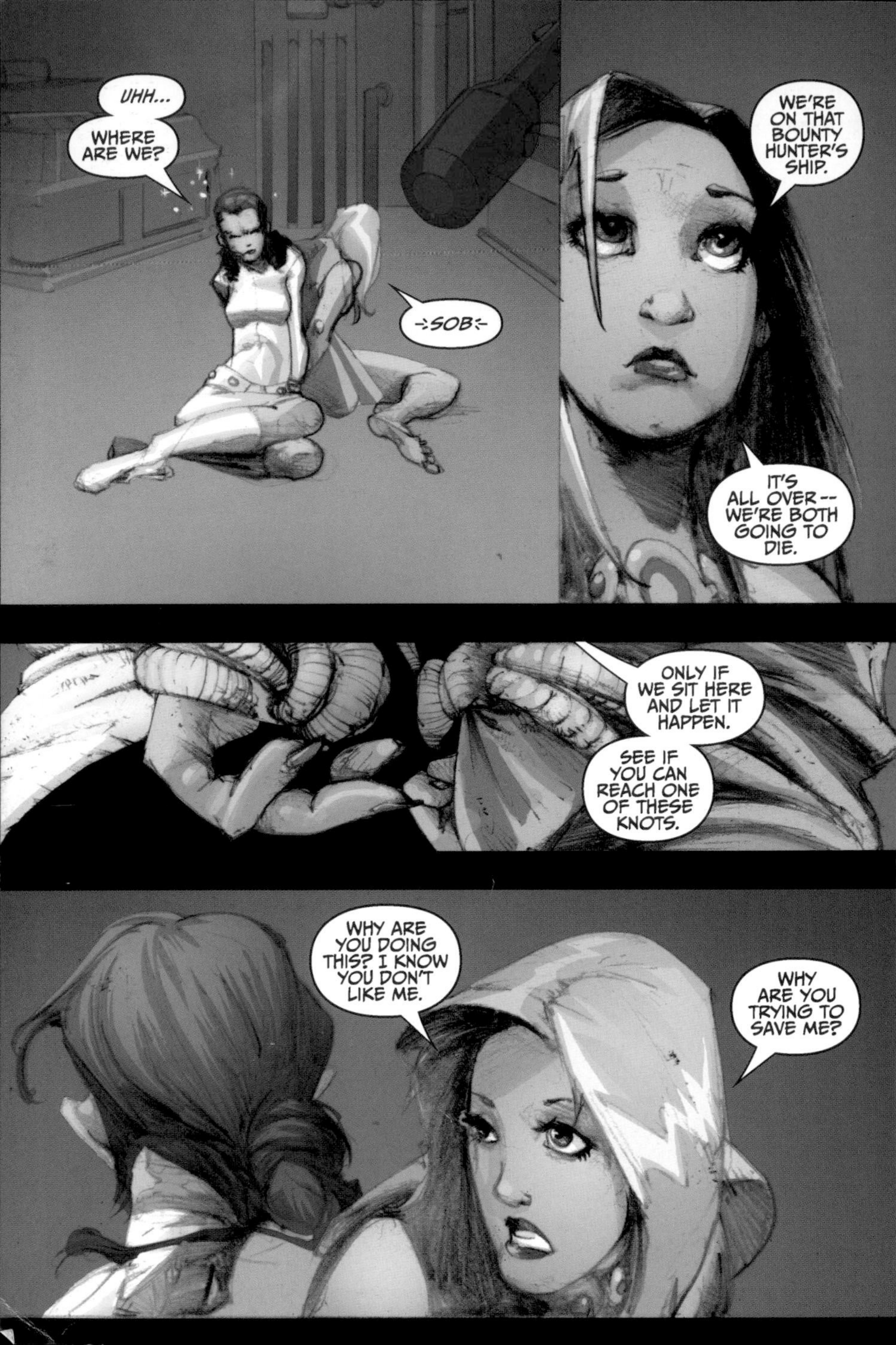
UHH...
WHERE ARE WE?
-:-SOB-:-
WE'RE ON THAT BOUNTY HUNTER'S SHIP.
IT'S ALL OVER-- WE'RE BOTH GOING TO DIE.
ONLY IF WE SIT HERE AND LET IT HAPPEN.
SEE IF YOU CAN REACH ONE OF THESE KNOTS.
WHY ARE YOU DOING THIS? I KNOW YOU DON'T LIKE ME.
WHY ARE YOU TRYING TO SAVE ME?

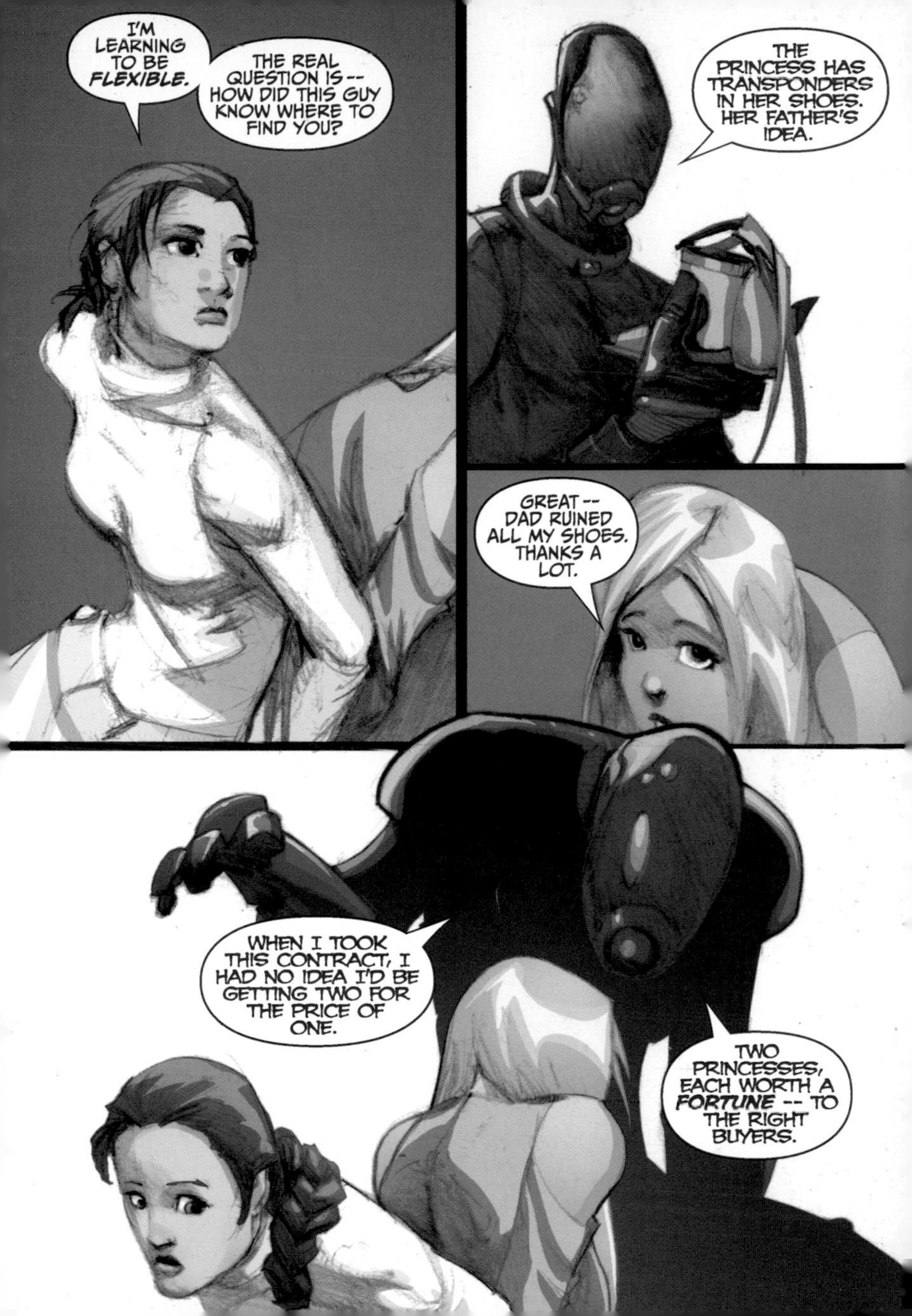
I'M LEARNING TO BE FLEXIBLE.
THE REAL QUESTION IS -- HOW DID THIS GUY KNOW WHERE TO FIND YOU?
THE PRINCESS HAS TRANSPONDERS IN HER SHOES. HER FATHER'S IDEA.
GREAT -- DAD RUINED ALL MY SHOES. THANKS A LOT.
WHEN I TOOK THIS CONTRACT, I HAD NO IDEA I'D BE GETTING TWO FOR THE PRICE OF ONE.
TWO PRINCESSES, EACH WORTH A FORTUNE -- TO THE RIGHT BUYERS.

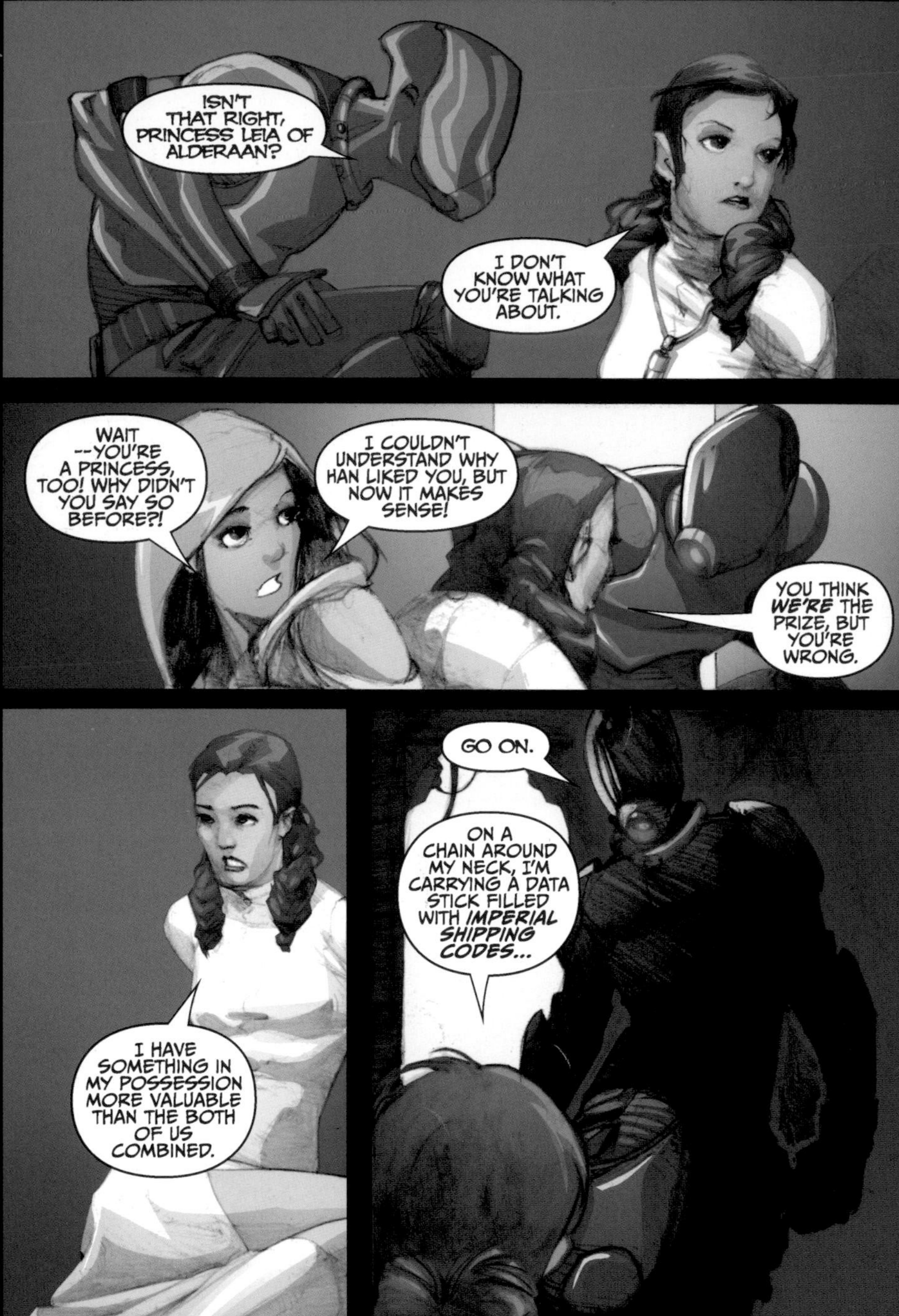
ISN'T THAT RIGHT, PRINCESS LEIA OF ALDERAAN?
I DON'T KNOW WHAT YOU'RE TALKING ABOUT.
WAIT --YOU'RE A PRINCESS, TOO! WHY DIDN'T YOU SAY SO BEFORE?!
I COULDN'T UNDERSTAND WHY HAN LIKED YOU, BUT NOW IT MAKES SENSE!
YOU THINK *WE'RE* THE PRIZE, BUT YOU'RE WRONG.
I HAVE SOMETHING IN MY POSSESSION MORE VALUABLE THAN THE BOTH OF US COMBINED.
GO ON.
ON A CHAIN AROUND MY NECK, I'M CARRYING A DATA STICK FILLED WITH *IMPERIAL SHIPPING CODES...*

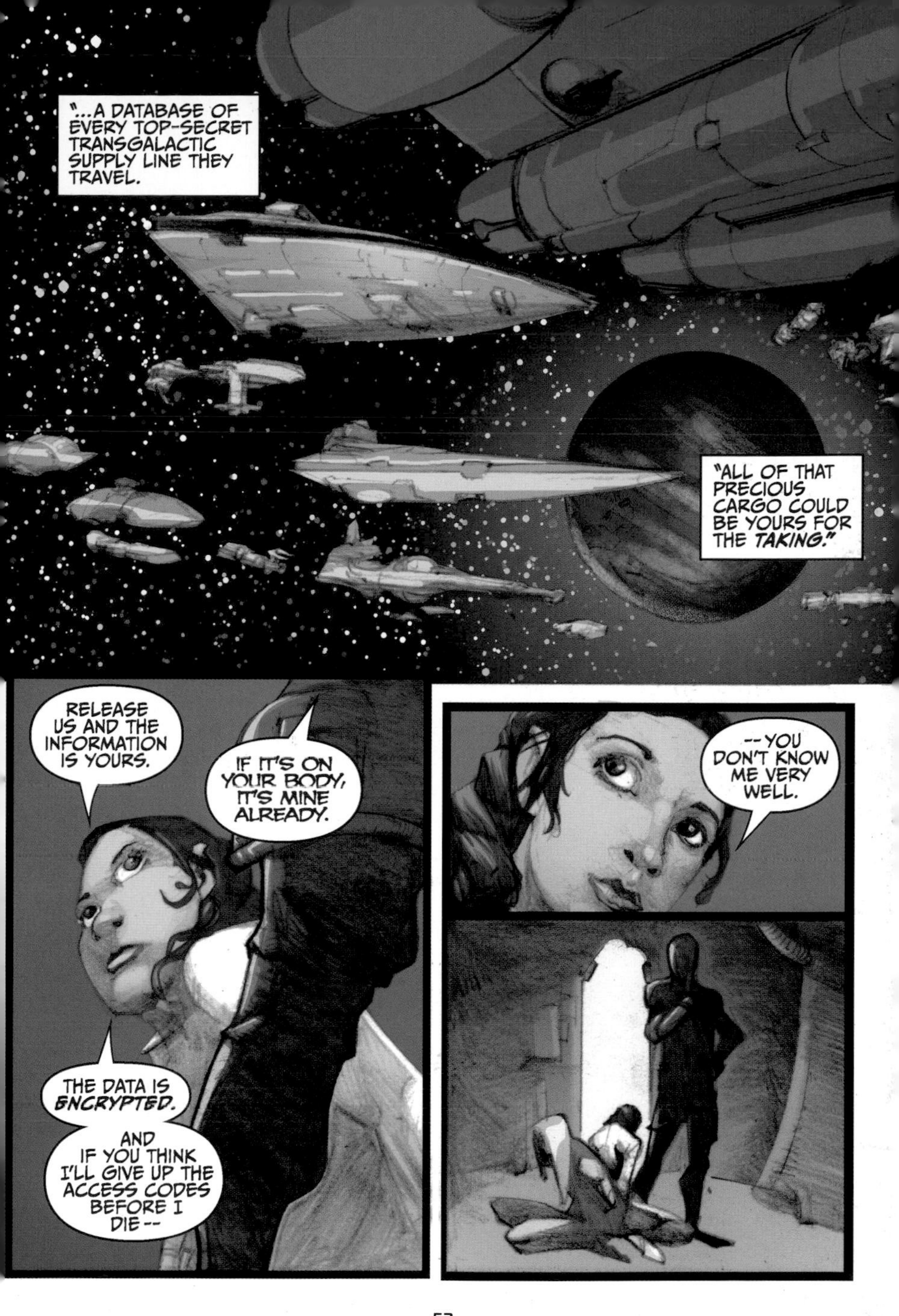
"...A DATABASE OF EVERY TOP-SECRET TRANSGALACTIC SUPPLY LINE THEY TRAVEL.
"ALL OF THAT PRECIOUS CARGO COULD BE YOURS FOR THE *TAKING*."
RELEASE US AND THE INFORMATION IS YOURS.
IF IT'S ON YOUR BODY, IT'S MINE ALREADY.
THE DATA IS *ENCRYPTED*.
AND IF YOU THINK I'LL GIVE UP THE ACCESS CODES BEFORE I DIE --
--YOU DON'T KNOW ME VERY WELL.

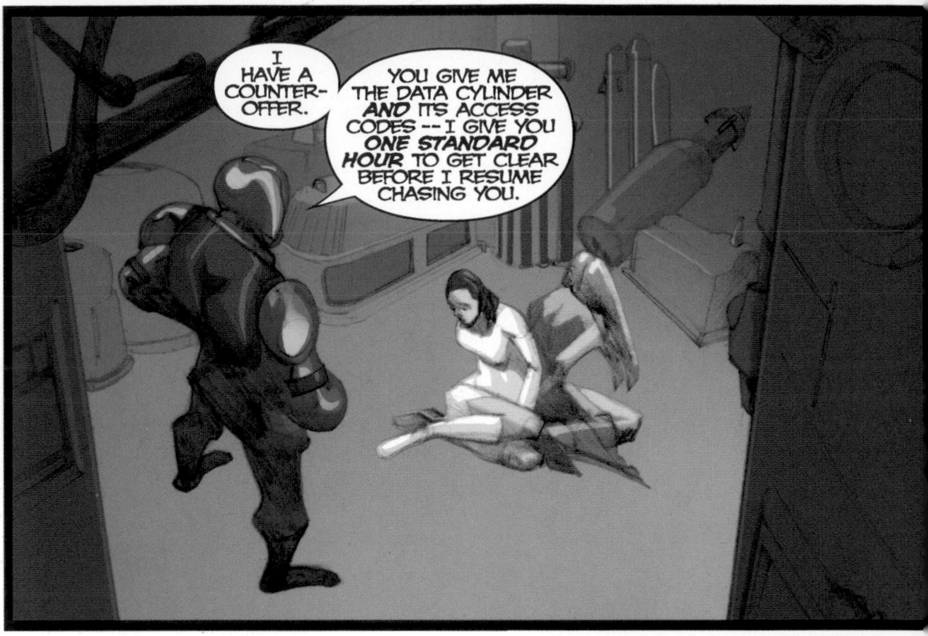
I HAVE A COUNTER-OFFER.
YOU GIVE ME THE DATA CYLINDER ***AND*** ITS ACCESS CODES -- I GIVE YOU ***ONE STANDARD HOUR*** TO GET CLEAR BEFORE I RESUME CHASING YOU.

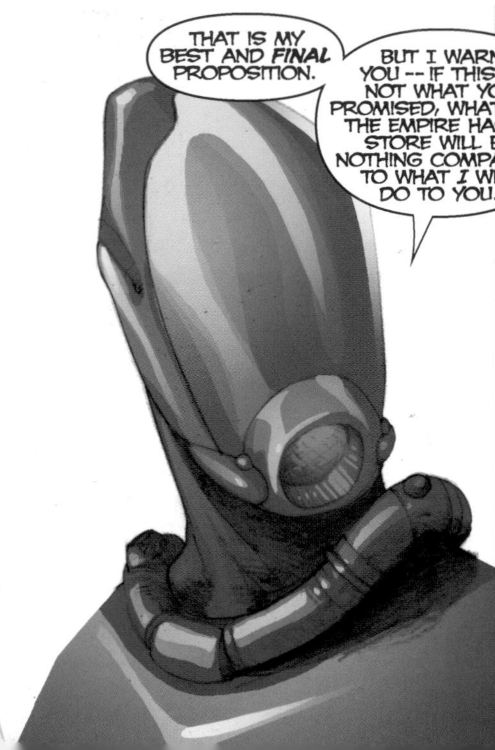
THAT IS MY BEST AND ***FINAL*** PROPOSITION.
BUT I WARN YOU -- IF THIS IS NOT WHAT YOU PROMISED, WHATEVER THE EMPIRE HAS IN STORE WILL BE NOTHING COMPARED TO WHAT *I* WILL DO TO YOU.

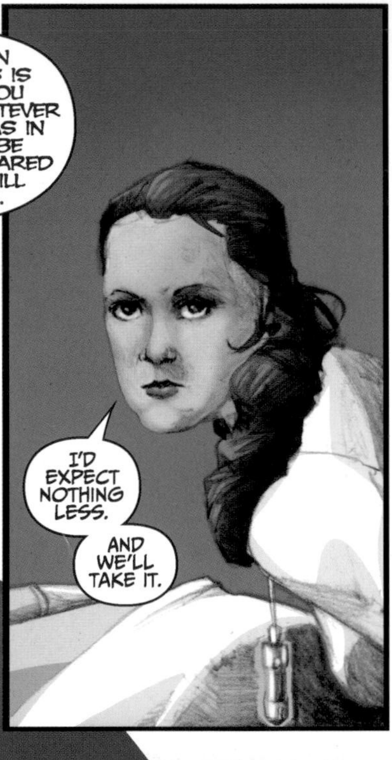
I'D EXPECT NOTHING LESS.
AND WE'LL TAKE IT.

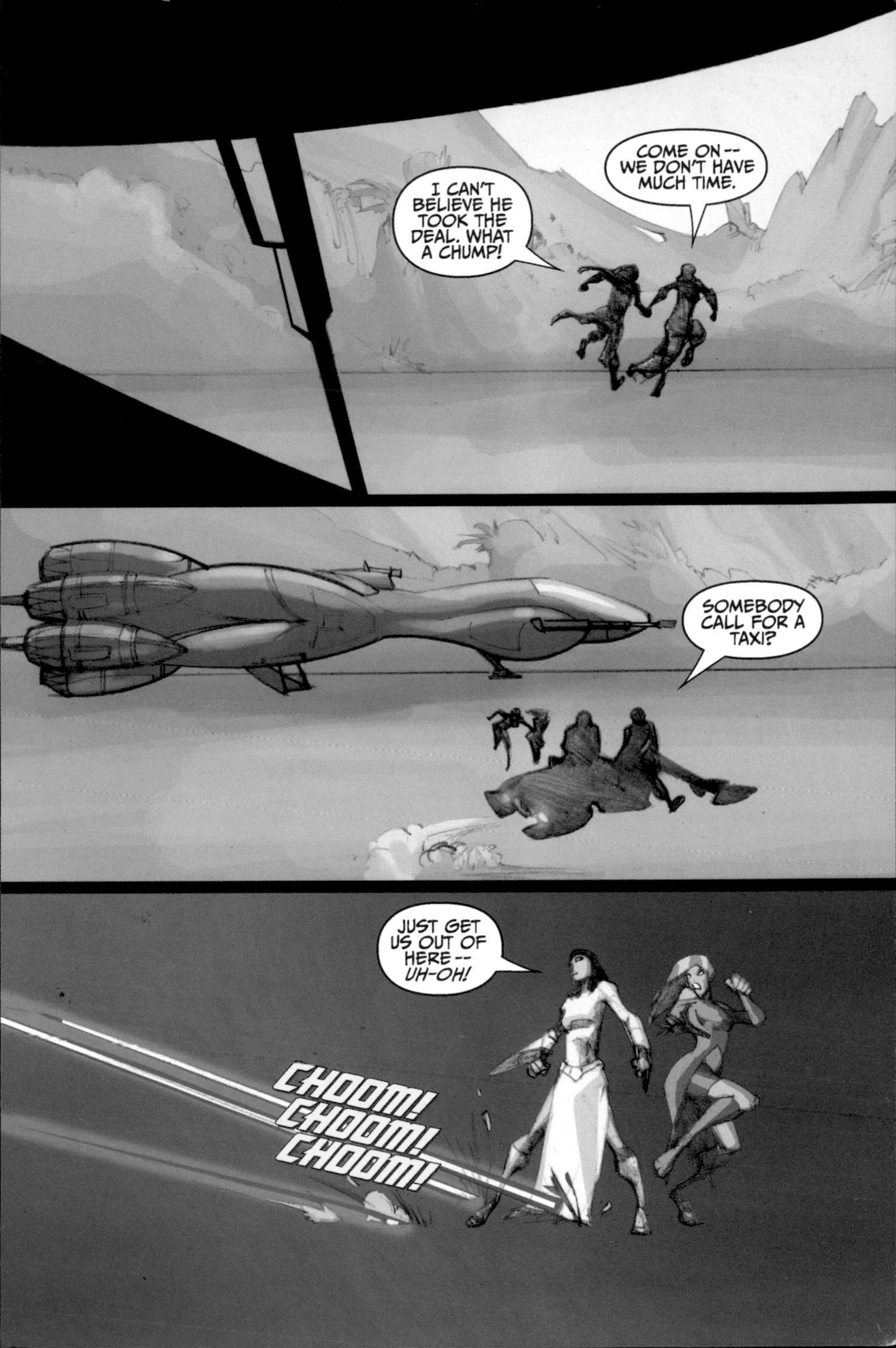
I CAN'T BELIEVE HE TOOK THE DEAL. WHAT A CHUMP!
COME ON -- WE DON'T HAVE MUCH TIME.
SOMEBODY CALL FOR A TAXI?
JUST GET US OUT OF HERE -- UH-OH!
CHOOM! CHOOM! CHOOM!

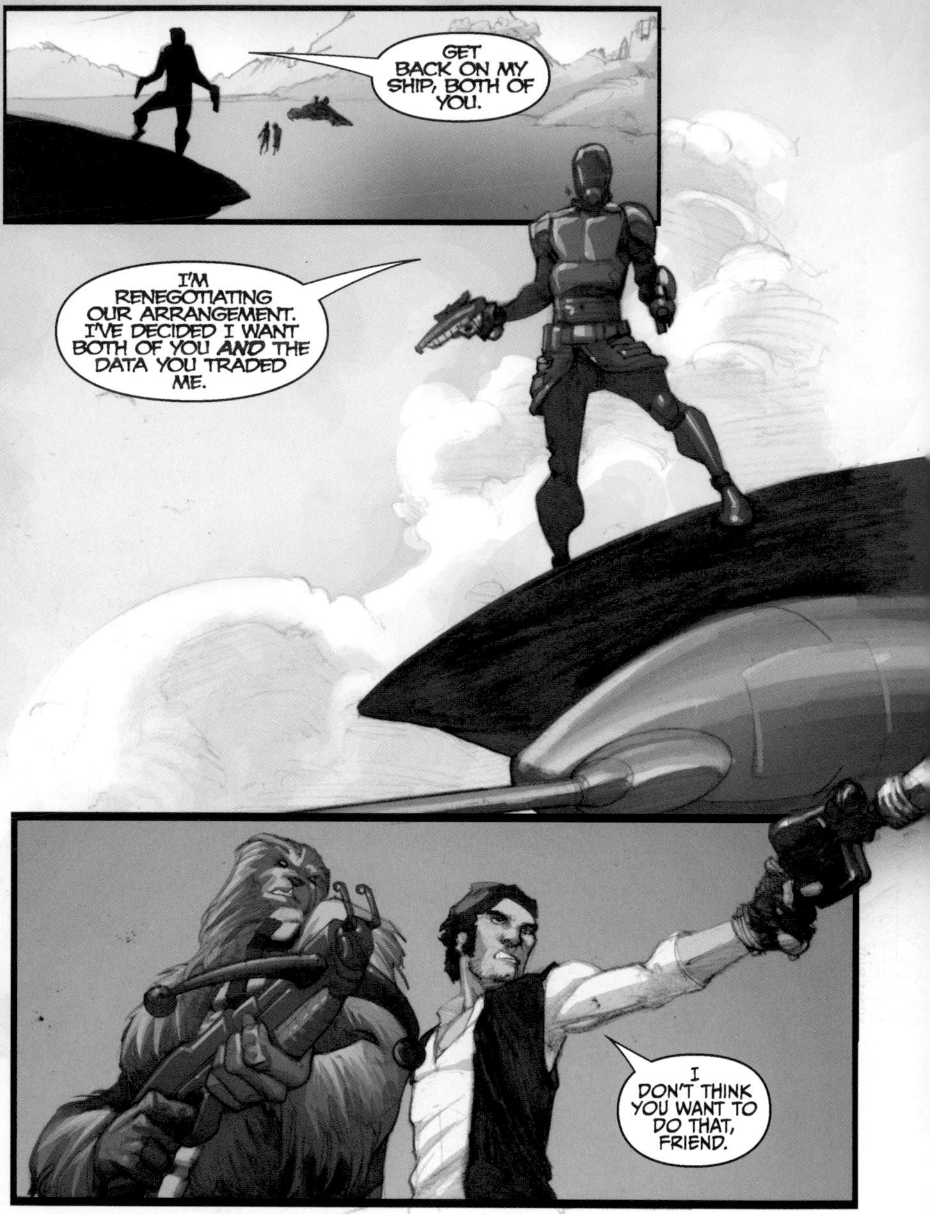
GET BACK ON MY SHIP, BOTH OF YOU.
I'M RENEGOTIATING OUR ARRANGEMENT. I'VE DECIDED I WANT BOTH OF YOU *AND* THE DATA YOU TRADED ME.
I DON'T THINK YOU WANT TO DO THAT, FRIEND.

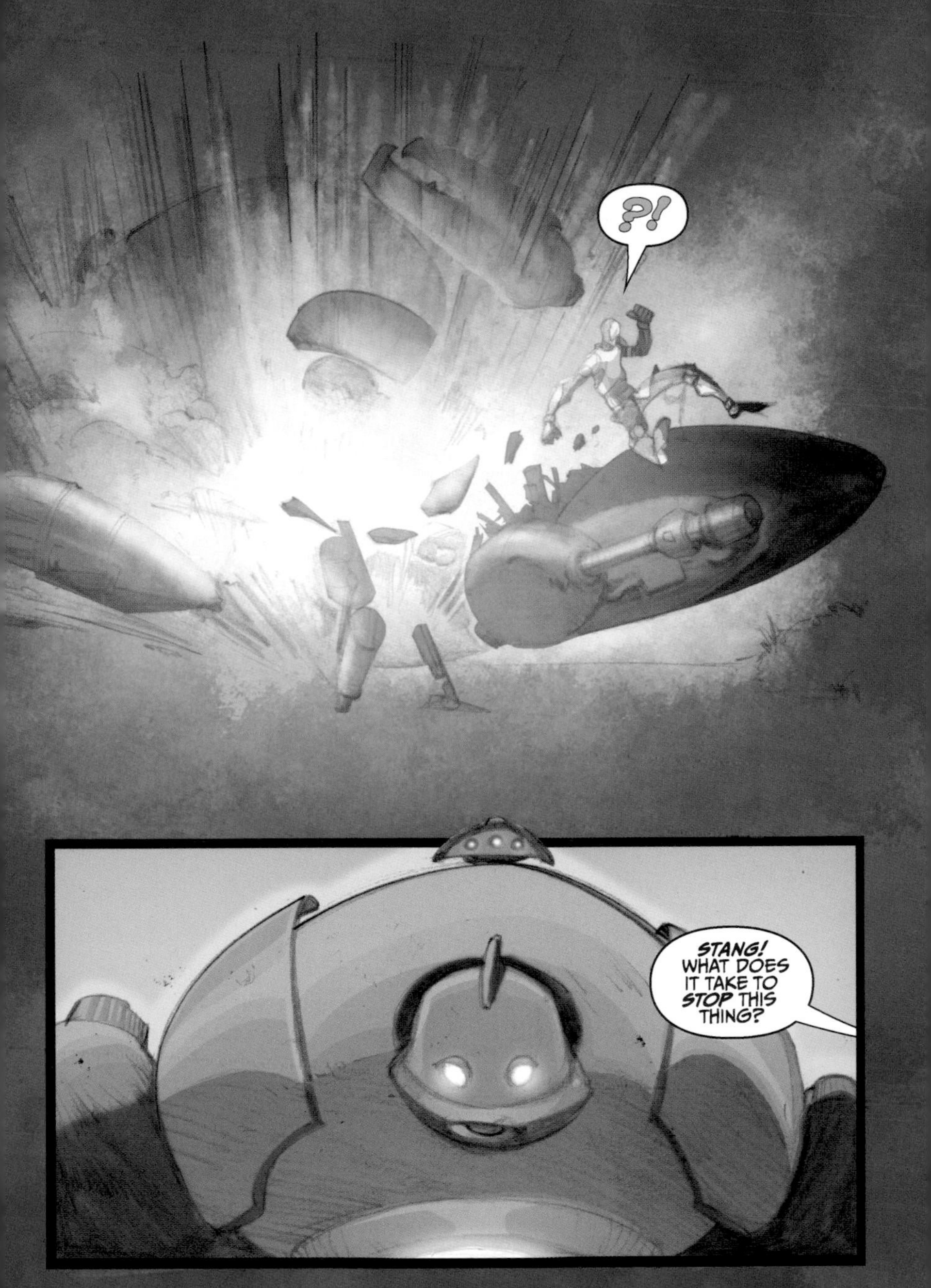
?!
STANG! WHAT DOES IT TAKE TO STOP THIS THING?

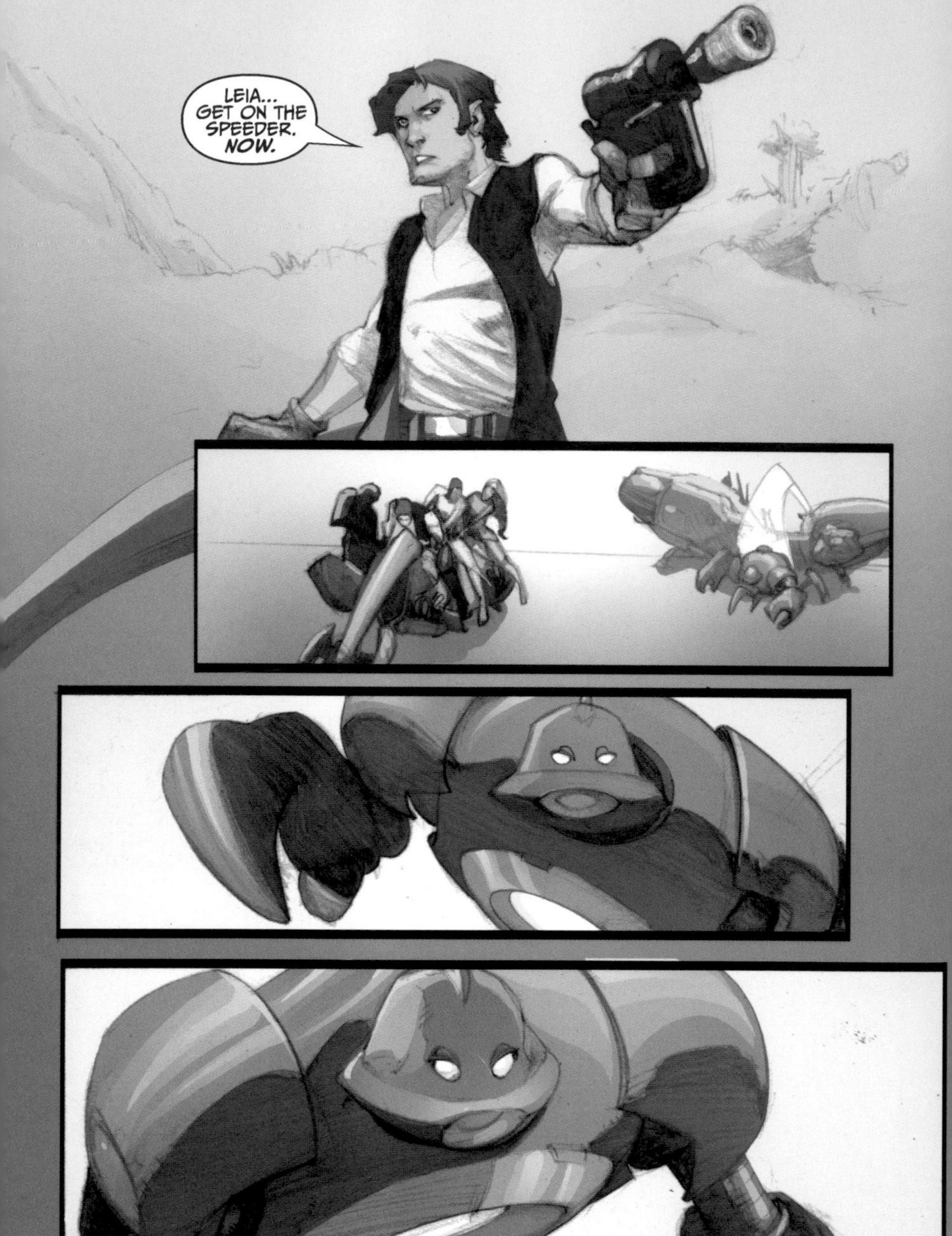
LEIA... GET ON THE SPEEDER. NOW.

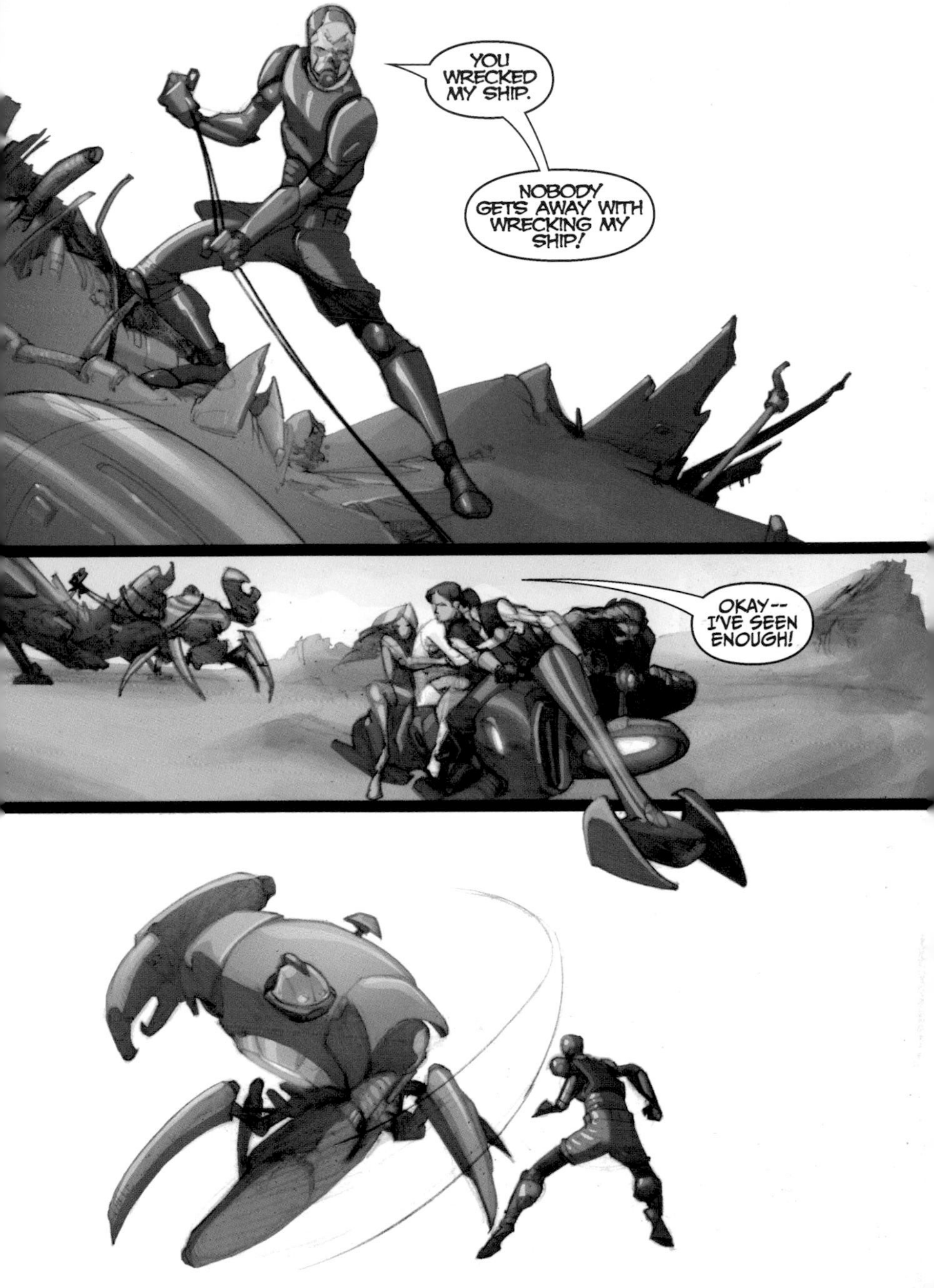
YOU WRECKED MY SHIP.
NOBODY GETS AWAY WITH WRECKING MY SHIP!
OKAY-- I'VE SEEN ENOUGH!

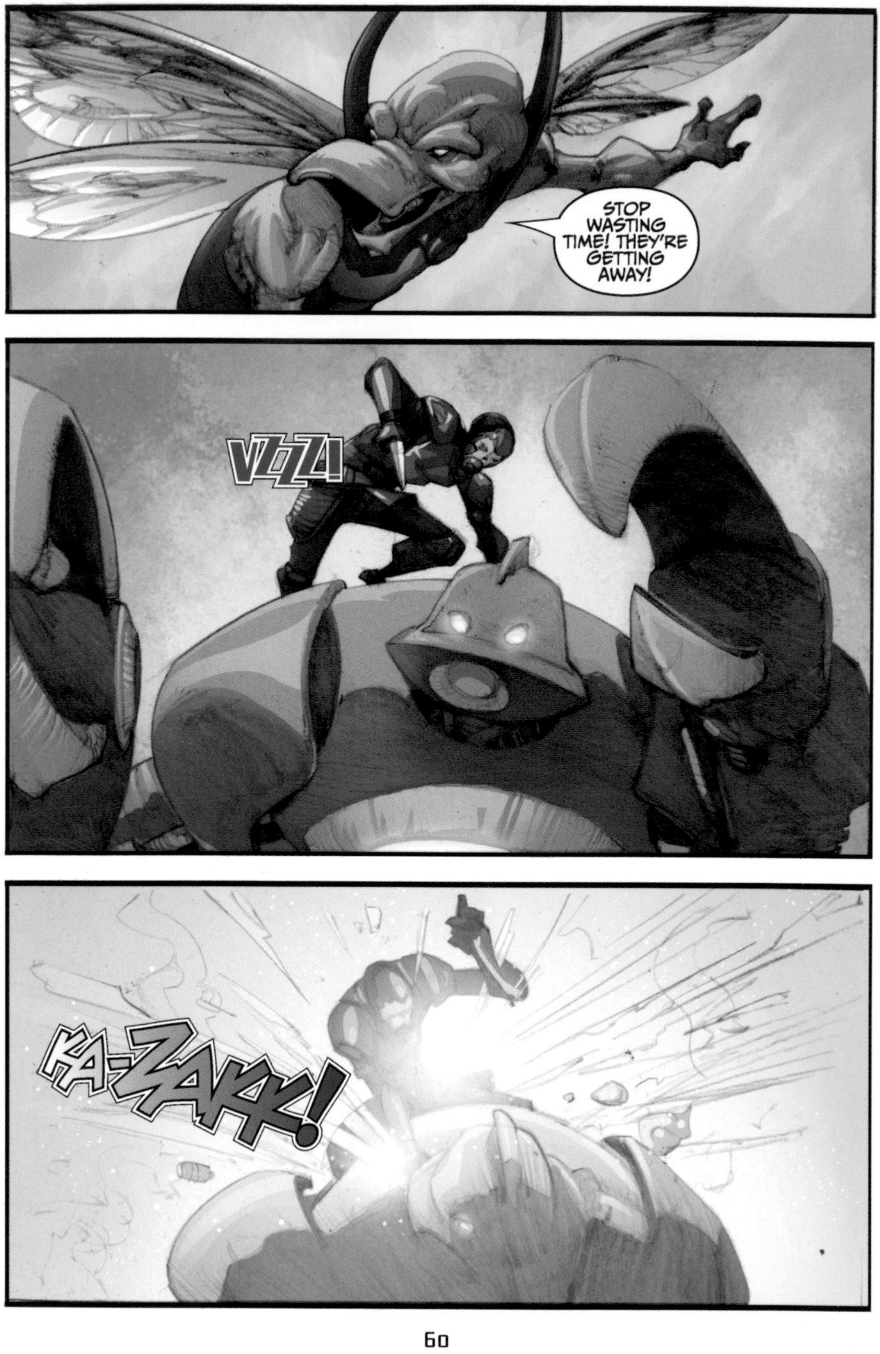
STOP WASTING TIME! THEY'RE GETTING AWAY!
VZZZ!
KA-ZAKK!

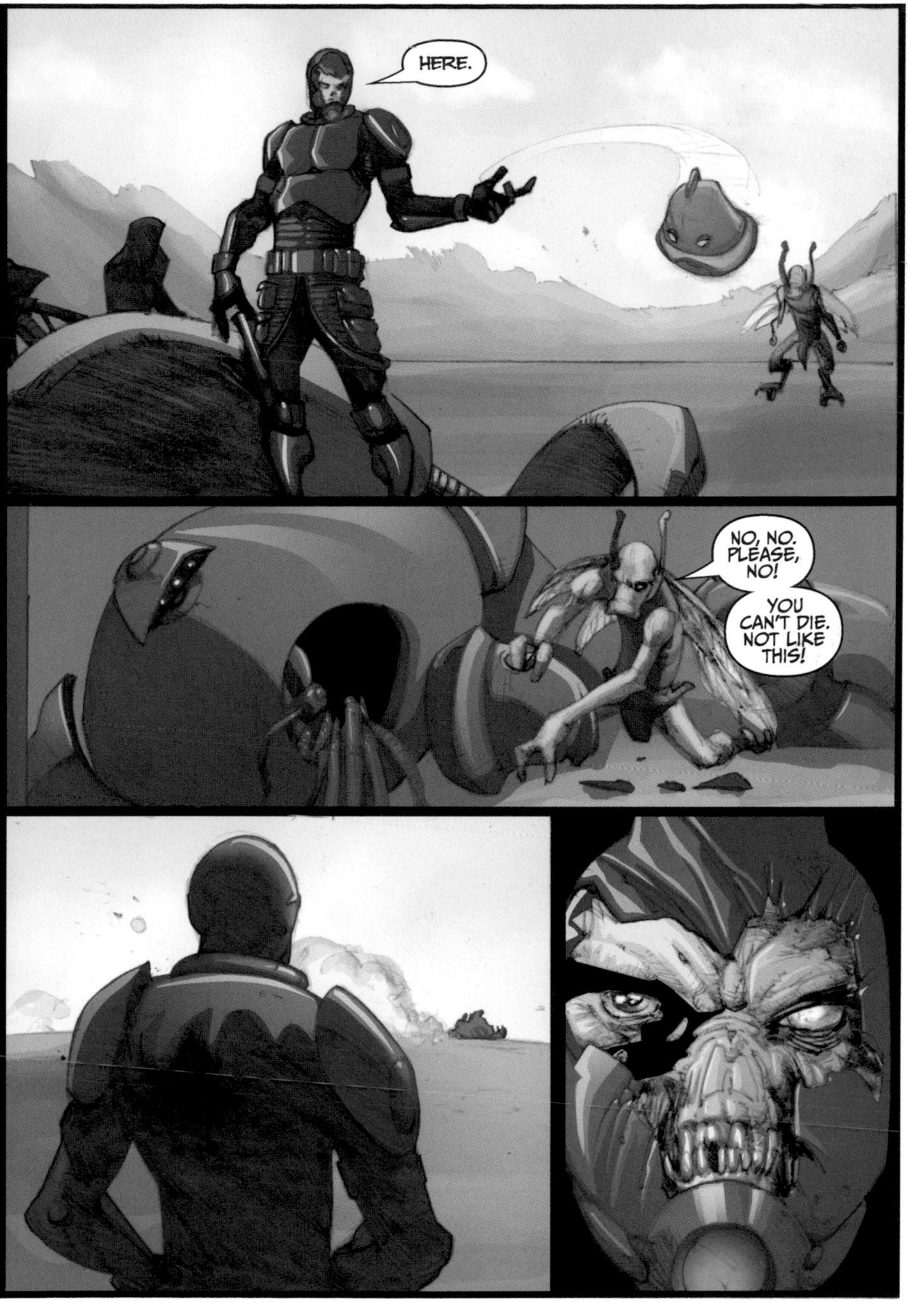
HERE.
NO, NO. PLEASE, NO!
YOU CAN'T DIE. NOT LIKE THIS!

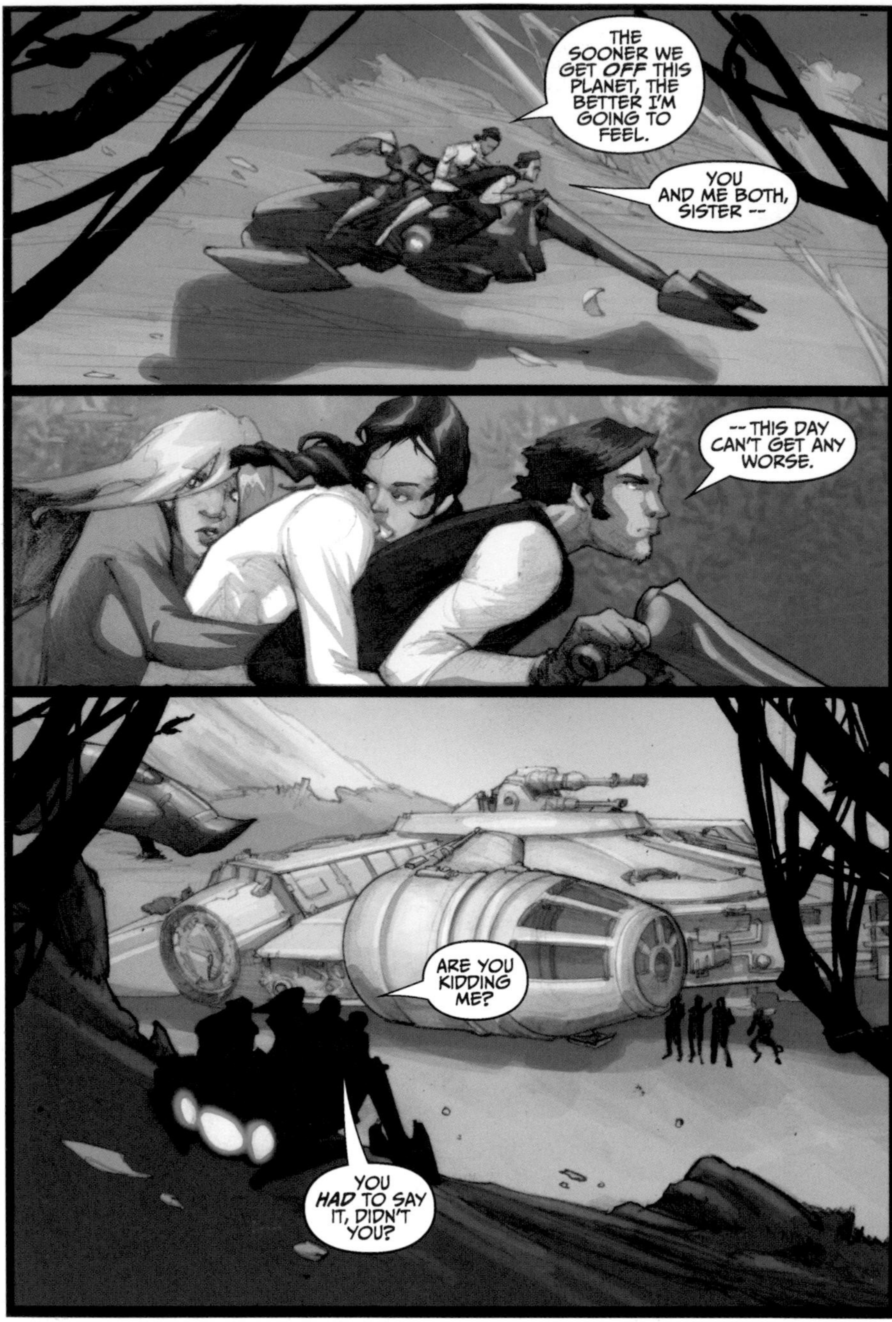
THE SOONER WE GET OFF THIS PLANET, THE BETTER I'M GOING TO FEEL.
YOU AND ME BOTH, SISTER --
-- THIS DAY CAN'T GET ANY WORSE.
ARE YOU KIDDING ME?
YOU HAD TO SAY IT, DIDN'T YOU?

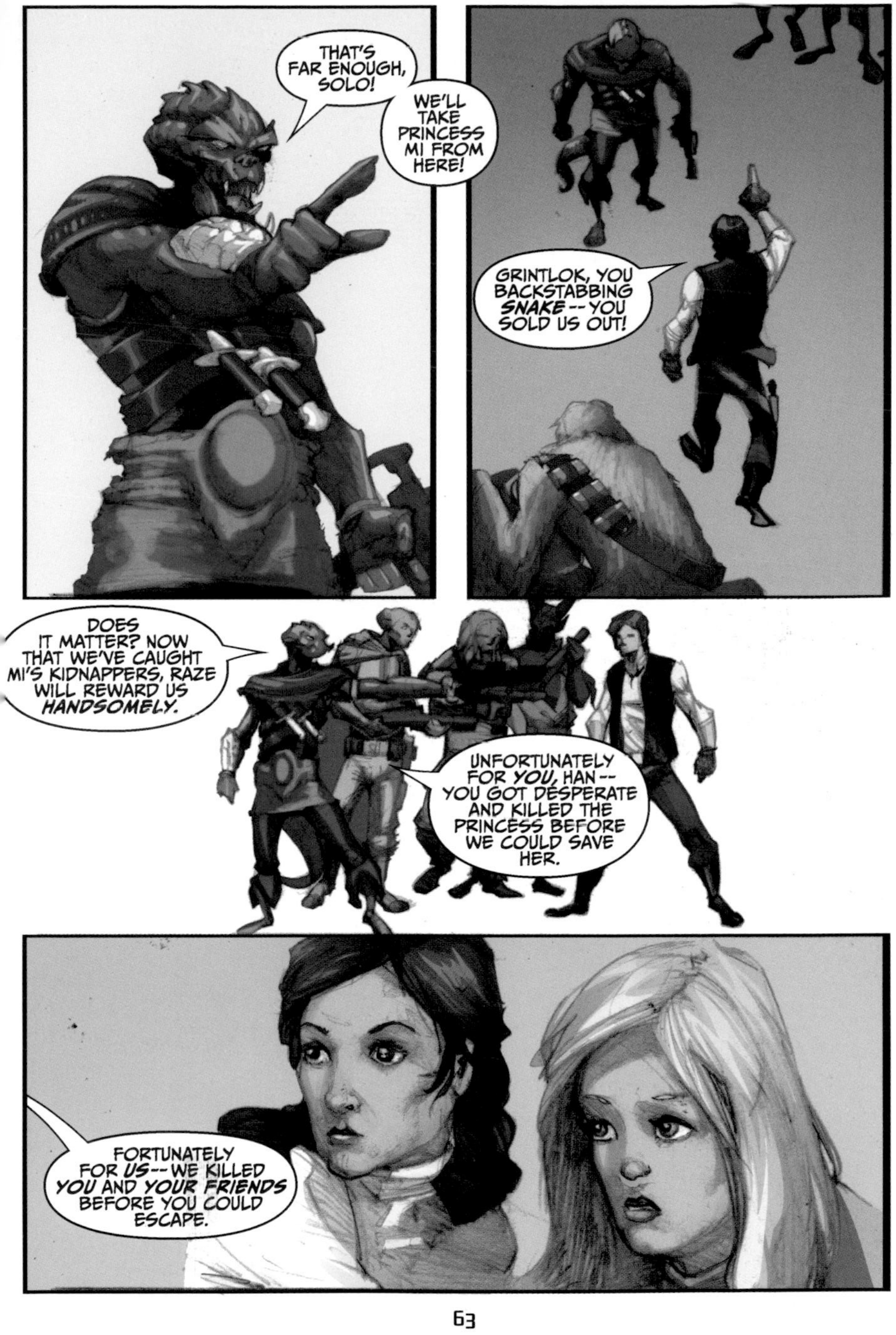
THAT'S FAR ENOUGH, SOLO!
WE'LL TAKE PRINCESS MI FROM HERE!
GRINTLOK, YOU BACKSTABBING SNAKE--YOU SOLD US OUT!
DOES IT MATTER? NOW THAT WE'VE CAUGHT MI'S KIDNAPPERS, RAZE WILL REWARD US HANDSOMELY.
UNFORTUNATELY FOR YOU, HAN--YOU GOT DESPERATE AND KILLED THE PRINCESS BEFORE WE COULD SAVE HER.
FORTUNATELY FOR US--WE KILLED YOU AND YOUR FRIENDS BEFORE YOU COULD ESCAPE.

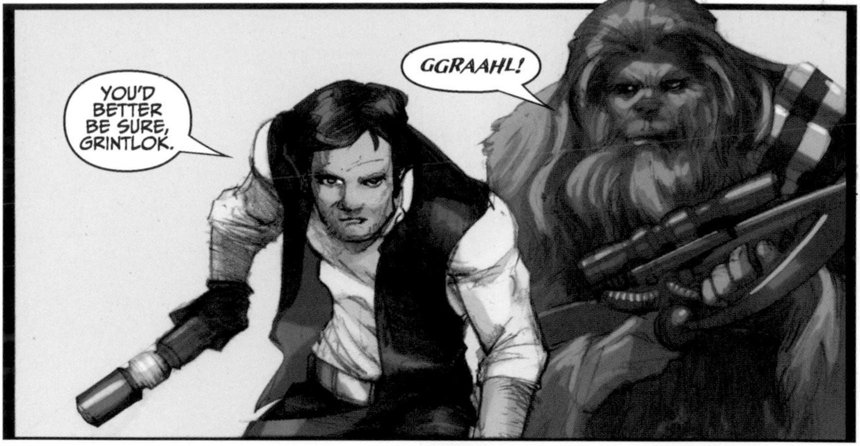
YOU'D BETTER BE SURE, GRINTLOK.
GGRAAHL!

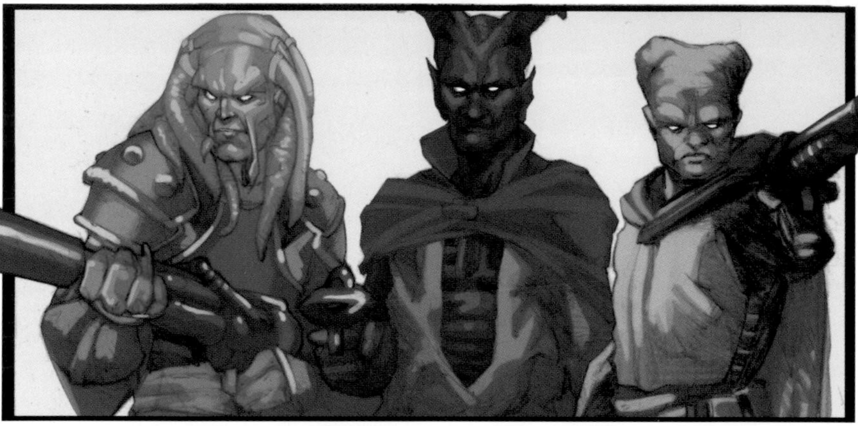

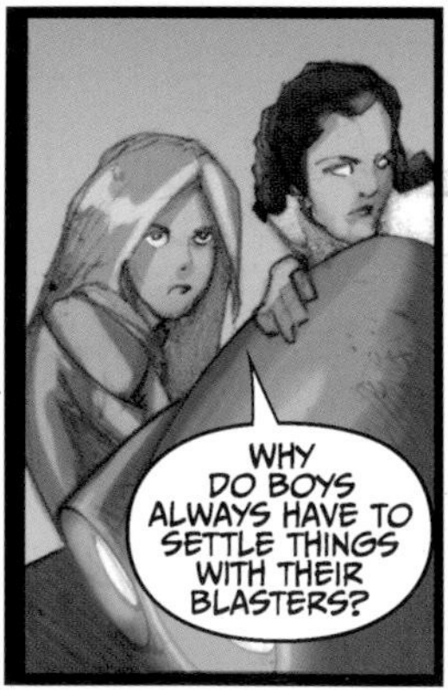
WHY DO BOYS ALWAYS HAVE TO SETTLE THINGS WITH THEIR BLASTERS?

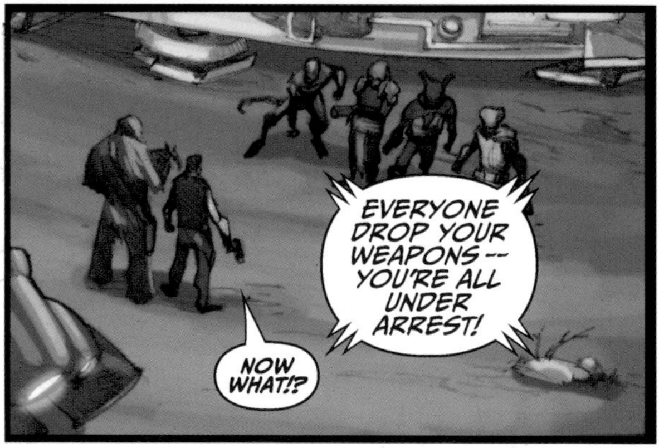
EVERYONE DROP YOUR WEAPONS -- YOU'RE ALL UNDER ARREST!
NOW WHAT!?

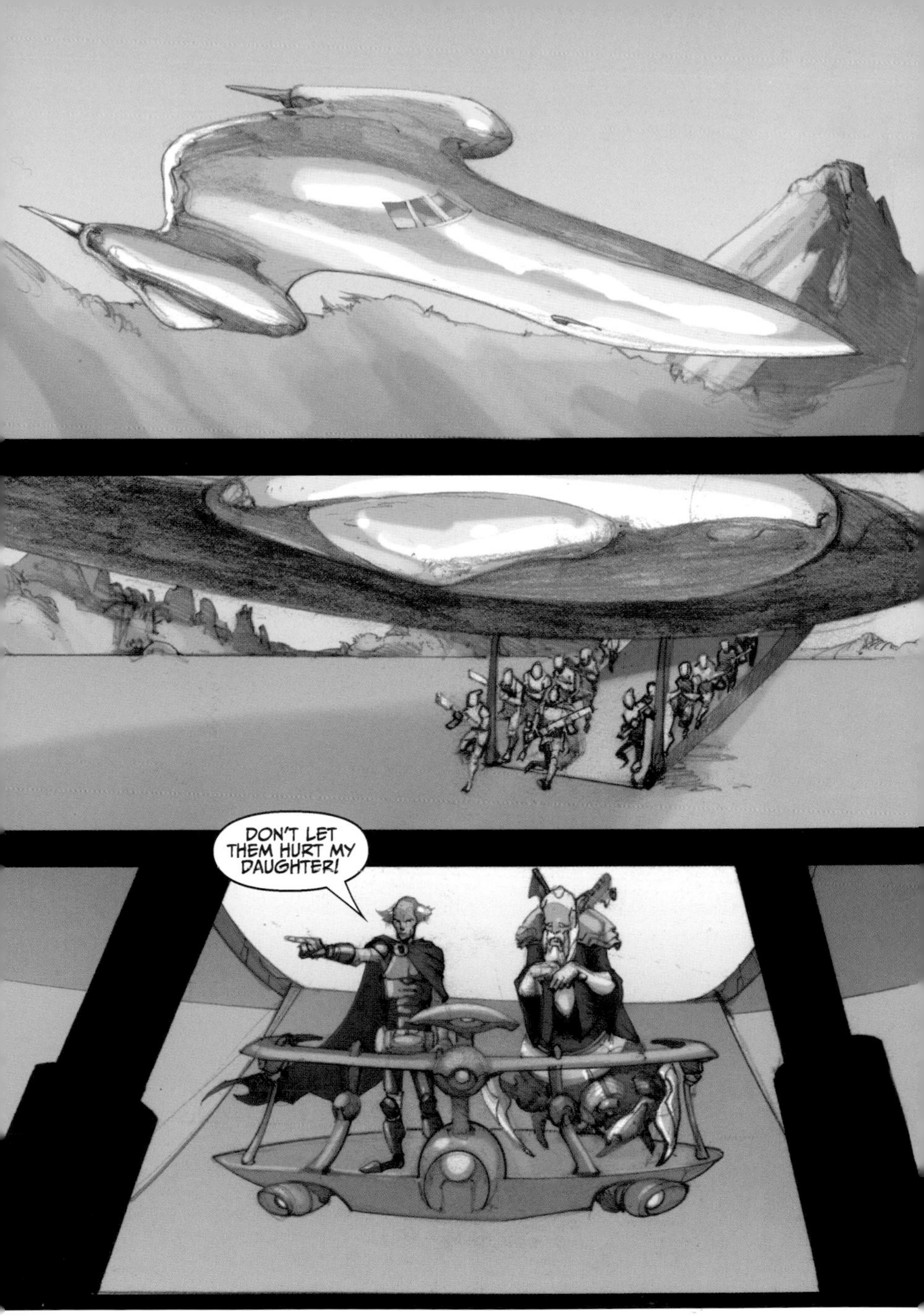
DON'T LET THEM HURT MY DAUGHTER!

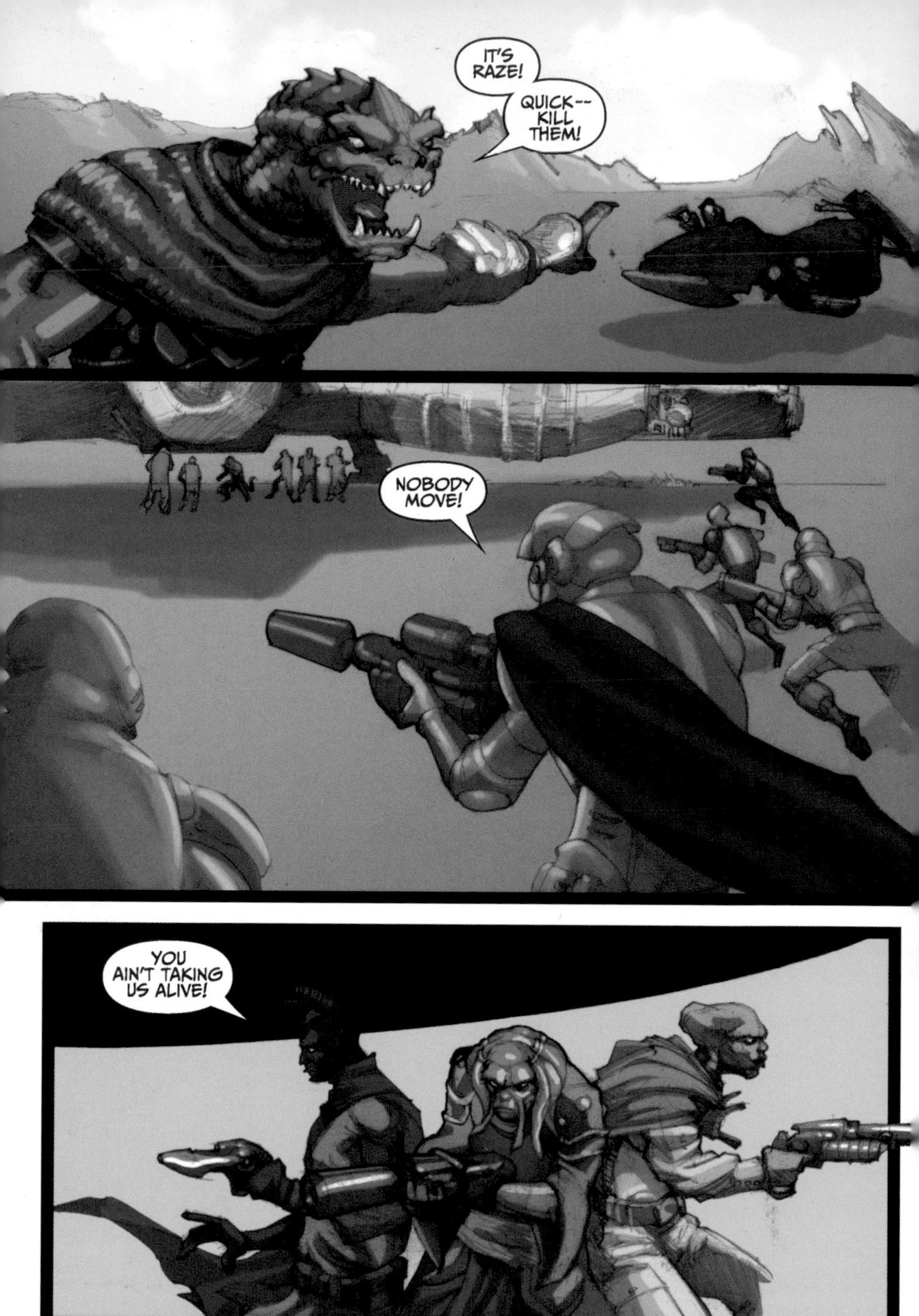
IT'S RAZE!
QUICK-- KILL THEM!
NOBODY MOVE!
YOU AIN'T TAKING US ALIVE!

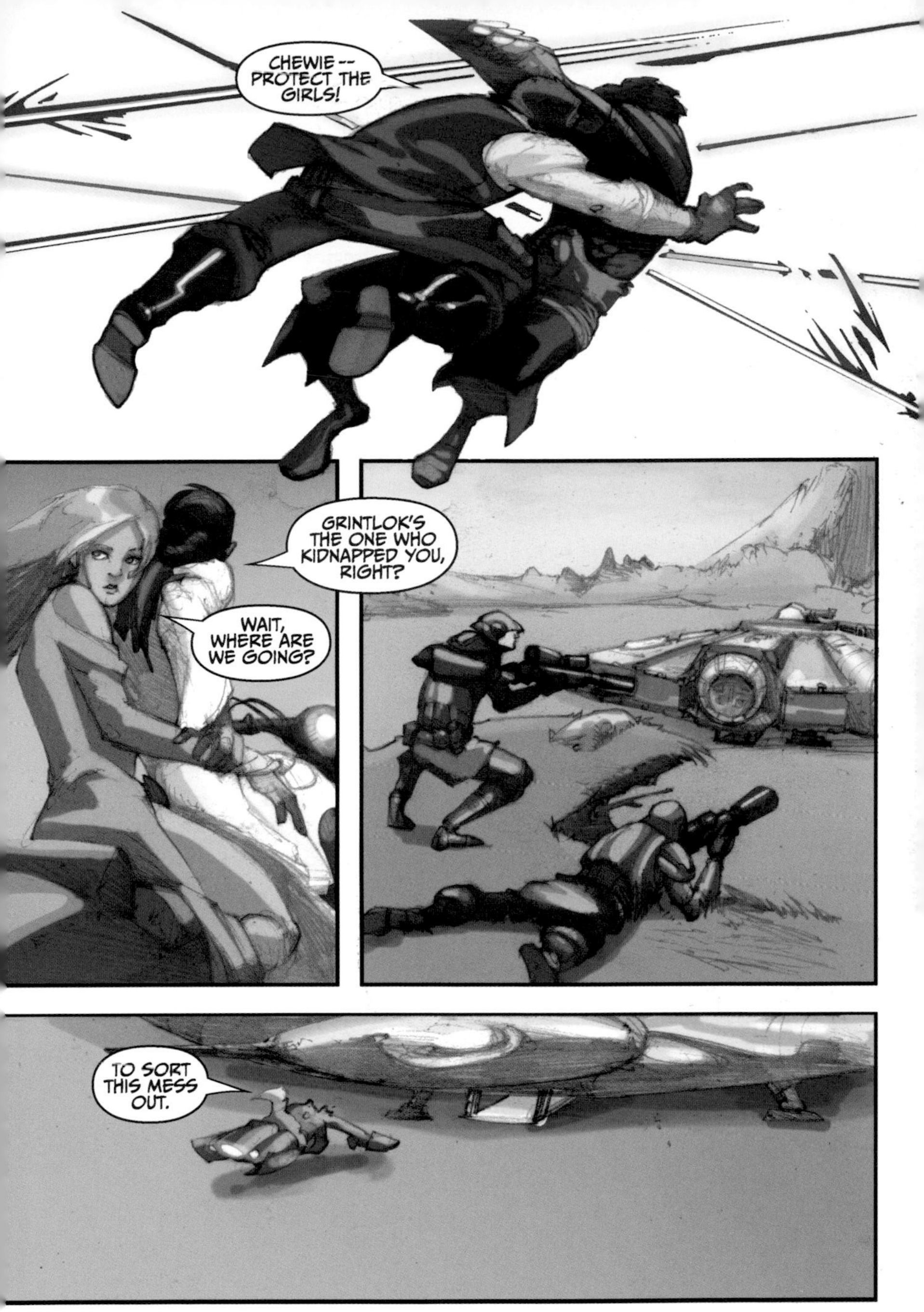
CHEWIE -- PROTECT THE GIRLS!
GRINTLOK'S THE ONE WHO KIDNAPPED YOU, RIGHT?
WAIT, WHERE ARE WE GOING?
TO SORT THIS MESS OUT.

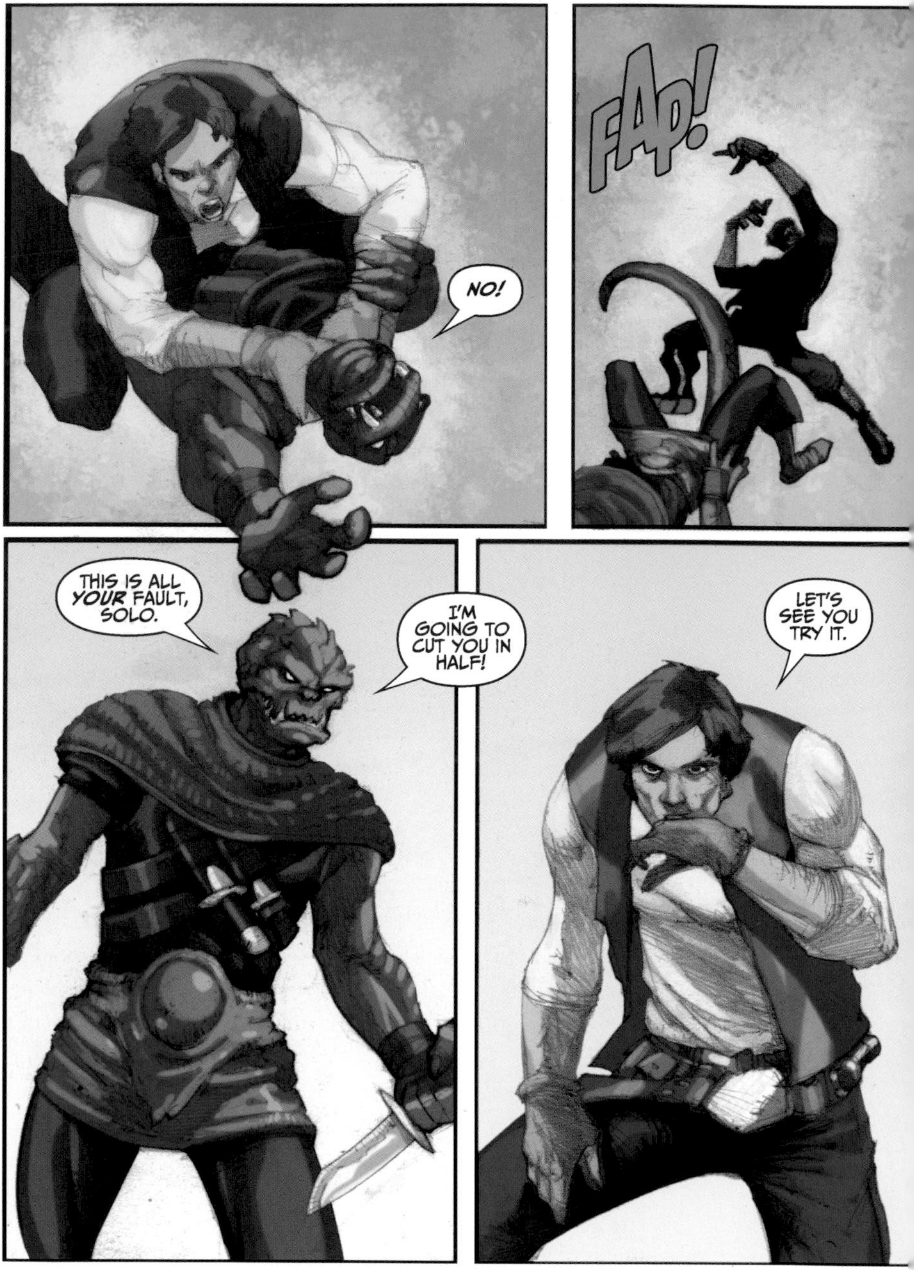
NO!
FAP!
THIS IS ALL YOUR FAULT, SOLO.
I'M GOING TO CUT YOU IN HALF!
LET'S SEE YOU TRY IT.

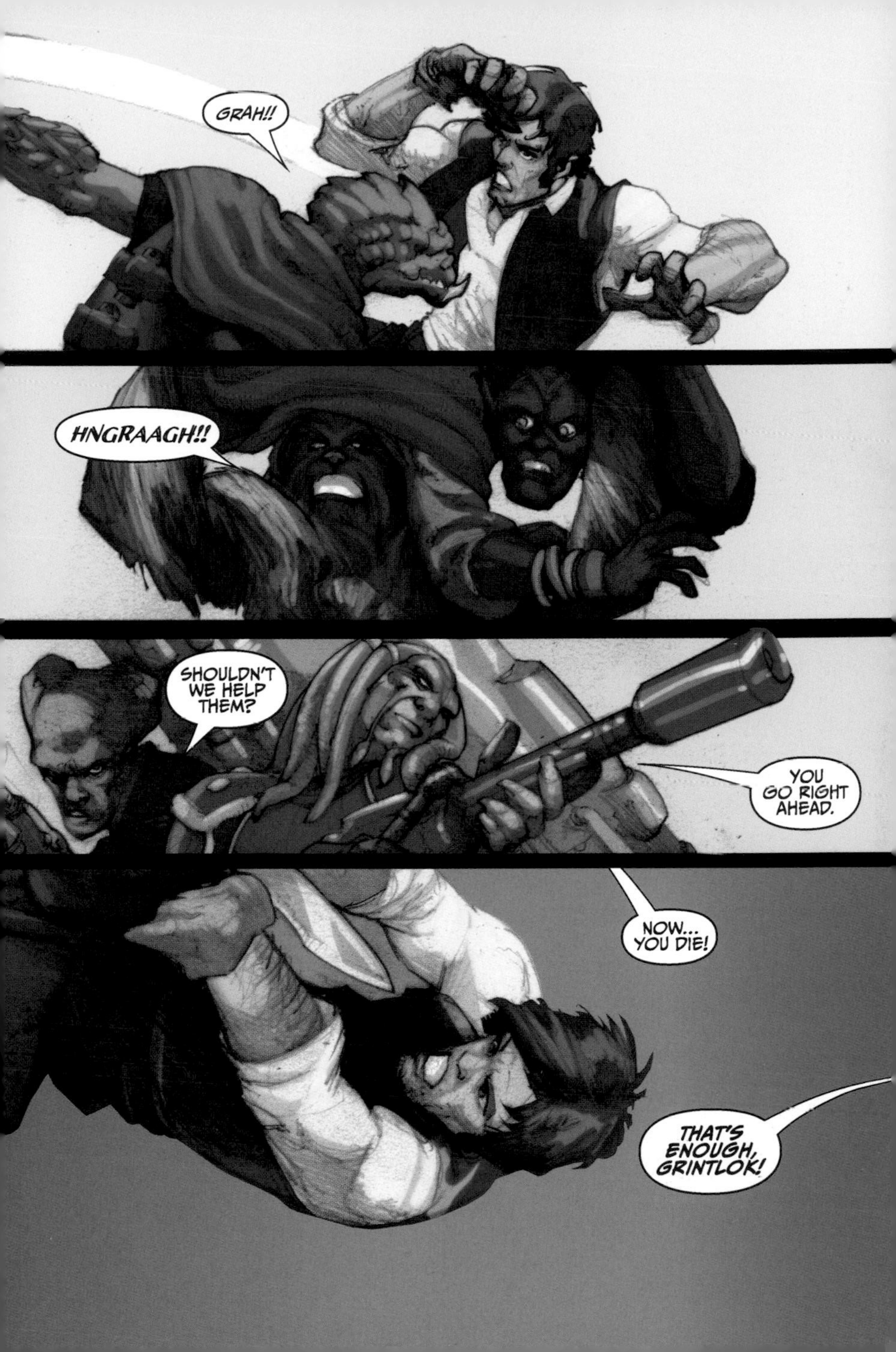
GRAH!!
HNGRAAGH!!
SHOULDN'T WE HELP THEM?
YOU GO RIGHT AHEAD.
NOW... YOU DIE!
THAT'S ENOUGH, GRINTLOK!

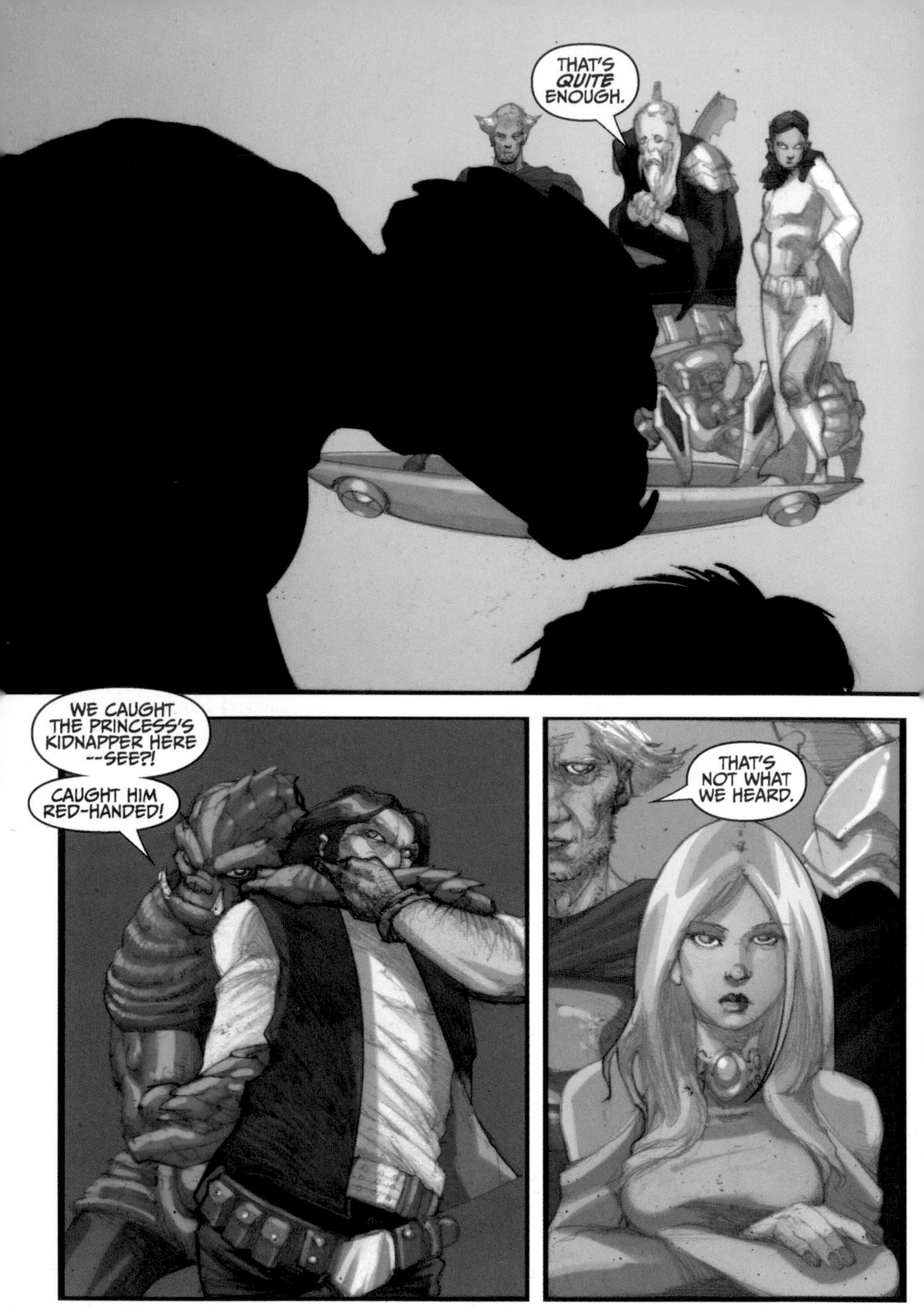
THAT'S QUITE ENOUGH.
WE CAUGHT THE PRINCESS'S KIDNAPPER HERE --SEE?!
CAUGHT HIM RED-HANDED!
THAT'S NOT WHAT WE HEARD.

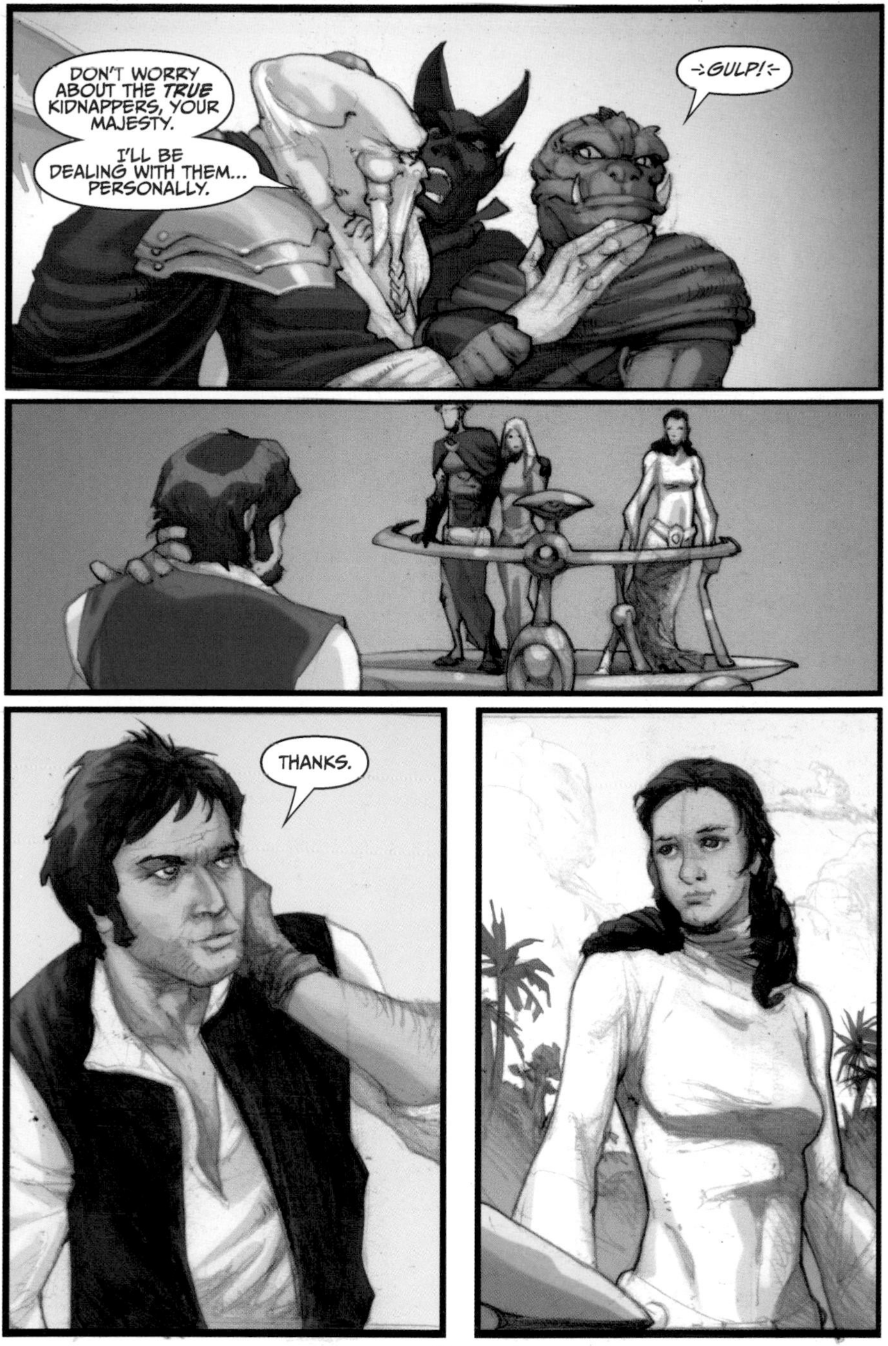
DON'T WORRY ABOUT THE TRUE KIDNAPPERS, YOUR MAJESTY.
I'LL BE DEALING WITH THEM... PERSONALLY.
-GULP!-
THANKS.

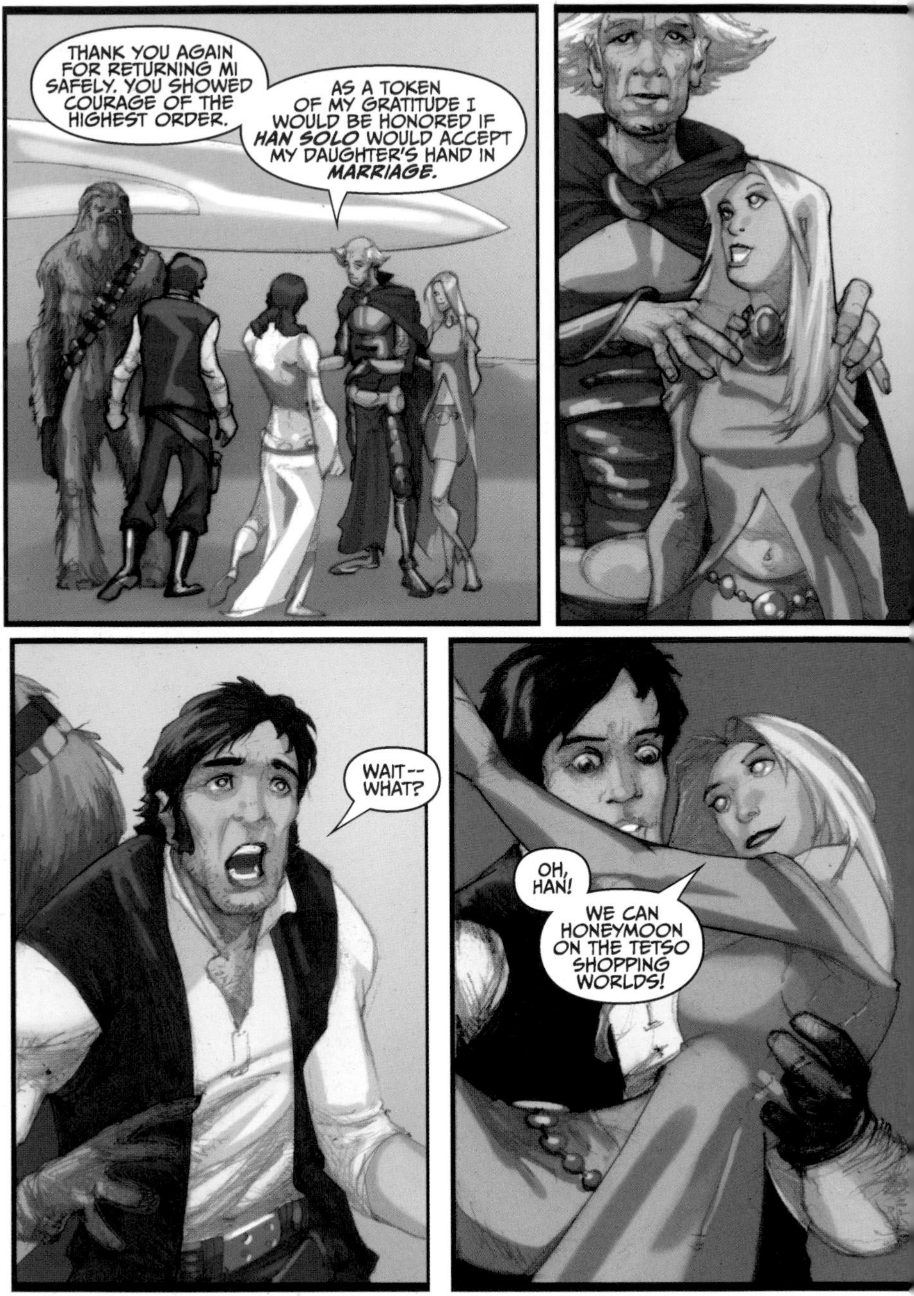
THANK YOU AGAIN FOR RETURNING MI SAFELY. YOU SHOWED COURAGE OF THE HIGHEST ORDER.
AS A TOKEN OF MY GRATITUDE I WOULD BE HONORED IF HAN SOLO WOULD ACCEPT MY DAUGHTER'S HAND IN MARRIAGE.
WAIT-- WHAT?
OH, HAN!
WE CAN HONEYMOON ON THE TETSO SHOPPING WORLDS!

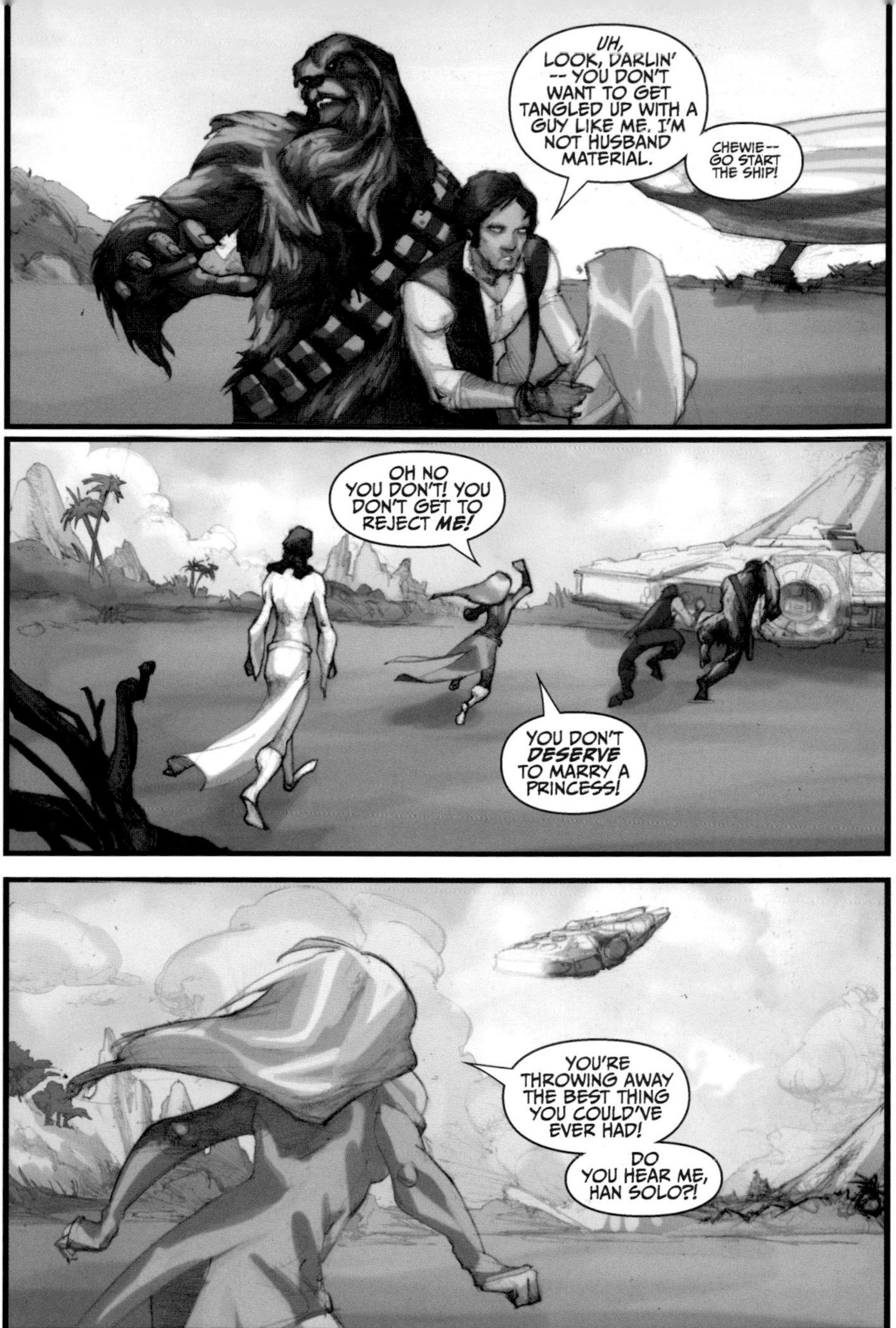
UH, LOOK, DARLIN' -- YOU DON'T WANT TO GET TANGLED UP WITH A GUY LIKE ME. I'M NOT HUSBAND MATERIAL.
CHEWIE-- GO START THE SHIP!
OH NO YOU DON'T! YOU DON'T GET TO REJECT *ME!*
YOU DON'T *DESERVE* TO MARRY A PRINCESS!
YOU'RE THROWING AWAY THE BEST THING YOU COULD'VE EVER HAD!
DO YOU HEAR ME, HAN SOLO?!

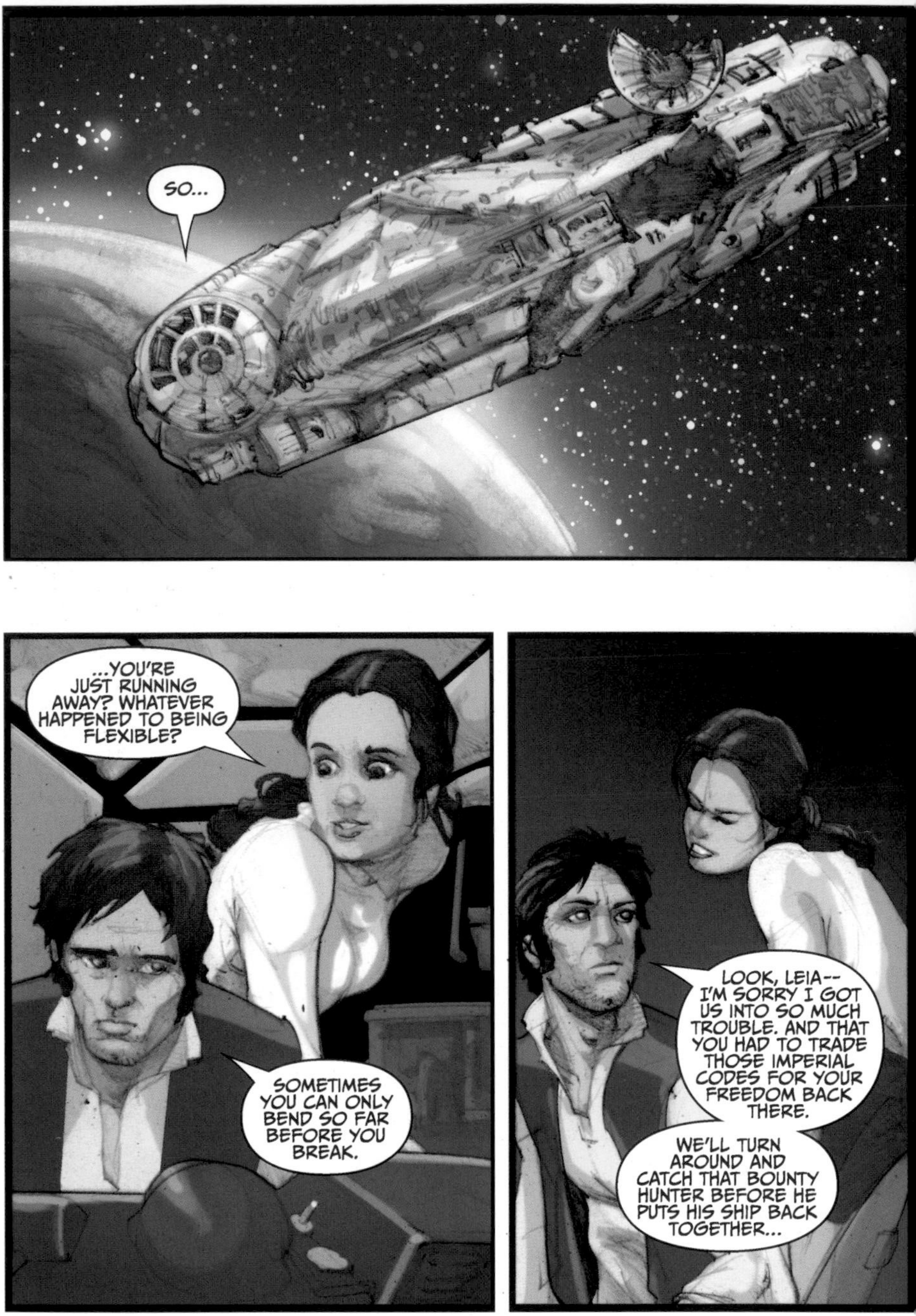
SO...
...YOU'RE JUST RUNNING AWAY? WHATEVER HAPPENED TO BEING FLEXIBLE?
SOMETIMES YOU CAN ONLY BEND SO FAR BEFORE YOU BREAK.
LOOK, LEIA-- I'M SORRY I GOT US INTO SO MUCH TROUBLE. AND THAT YOU HAD TO TRADE THOSE IMPERIAL CODES FOR YOUR FREEDOM BACK THERE.
WE'LL TURN AROUND AND CATCH THAT BOUNTY HUNTER BEFORE HE PUTS HIS SHIP BACK TOGETHER...

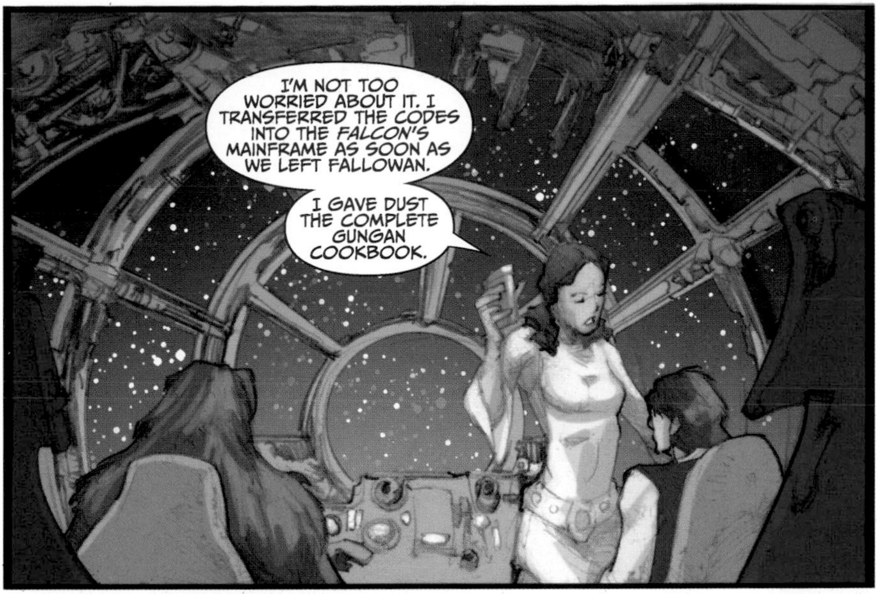
I'M NOT TOO WORRIED ABOUT IT. I TRANSFERRED THE CODES INTO THE *FALCON'S* MAINFRAME AS SOON AS WE LEFT FALLOWAN.
I GAVE DUST THE COMPLETE GUNGAN COOKBOOK.

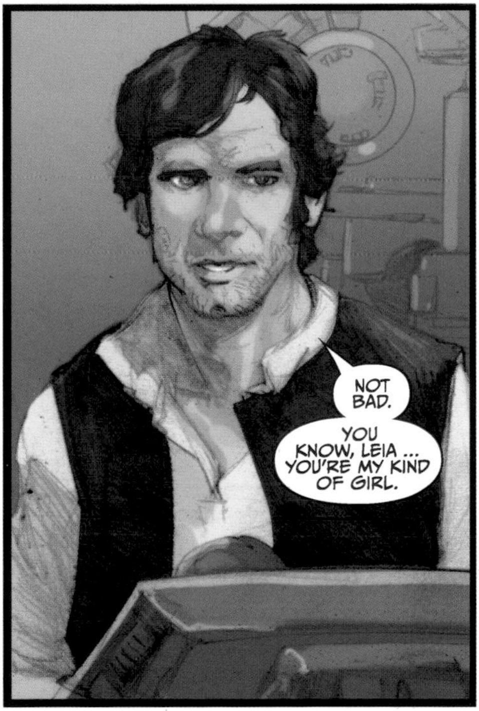
NOT BAD.
YOU KNOW, LEIA ... YOU'RE MY KIND OF GIRL.

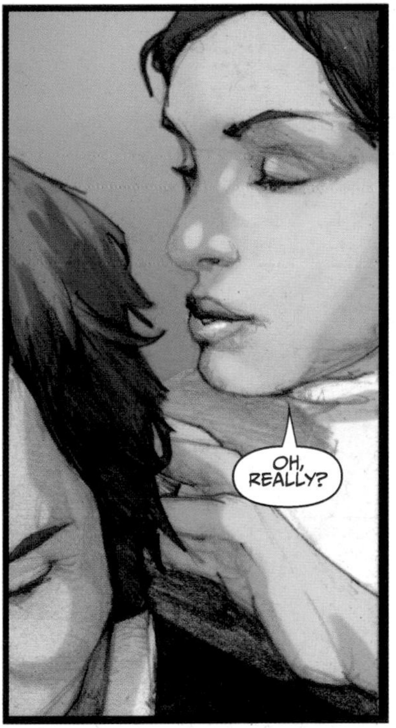
OH, REALLY?

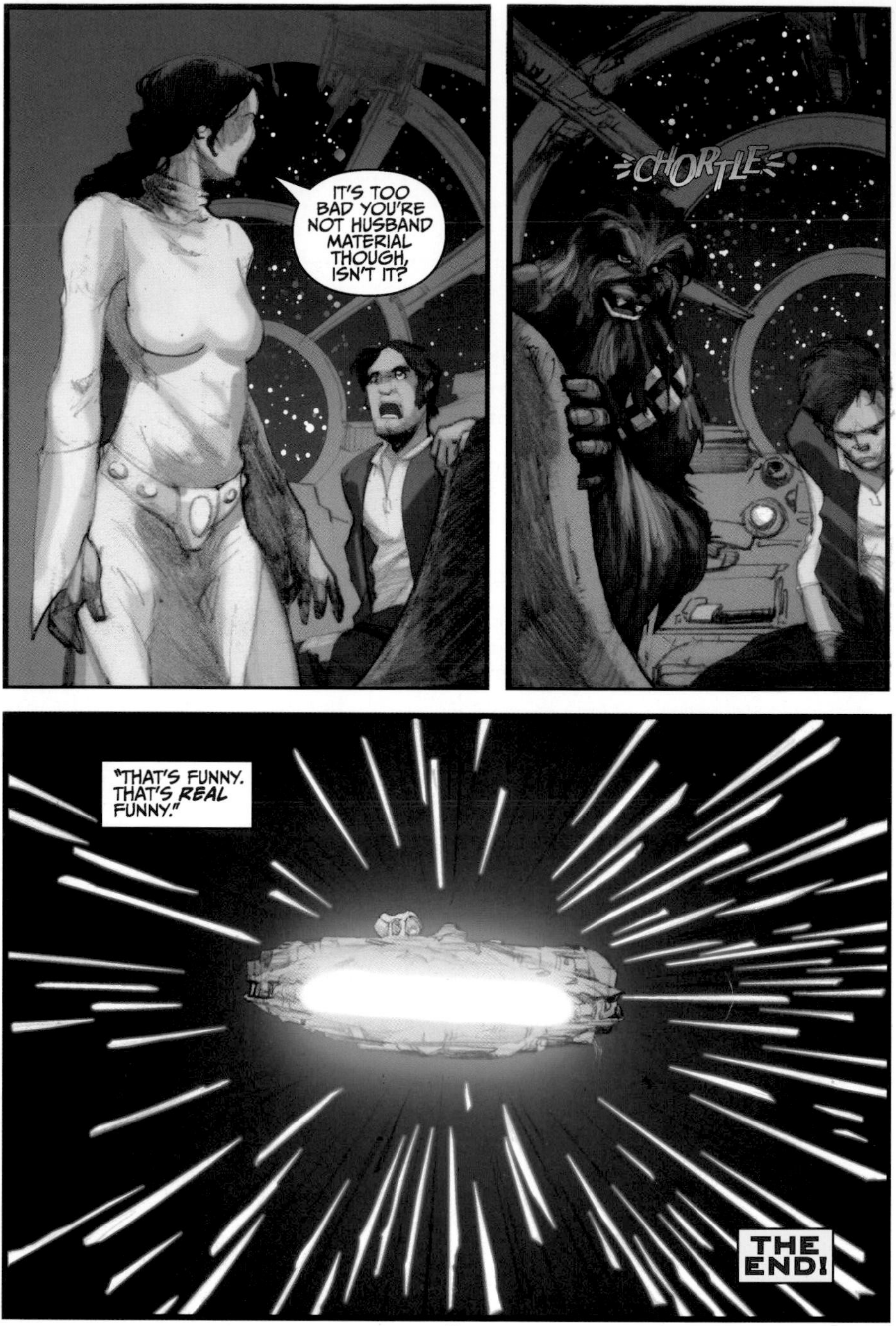
IT'S TOO BAD YOU'RE NOT HUSBAND MATERIAL THOUGH, ISN'T IT?
CHORTLE
"THAT'S FUNNY. THAT'S *REAL* FUNNY."
THE END!

President and Publisher **Mike Richardson**

Executive Vice President **Neil Hankerson**

Chief Financial Officer **Tom Weddle**

Vice President of Publishing **Randy Stradley**

Vice President of Business Development **Michael Martens**

Vice President of Marketing, Sales, and Licensing **Anita Nelson**

Vice President of Product Development **David Scroggy**

Vice President of Information Technology **Dale LaFountain**

Director of Purchasing **Darlene Vogel**

General Counsel **Ken Lizzi**

Editorial Director **Davey Estrada**

Senior Managing Editor **Scott Allie**

Senior Books Editor, Dark Horse Books **Chris Warner**

Executive Editor **Diana Schutz**

Director of Design and Production **Cary Grazzini**

Art Director **Lia Ribacchi**

Director of Scheduling **Cara Niece**

STAR WARS GRAPHIC NOVEL TIMELINE (IN YEARS)

Omnibus: Tales of the Jedi—5,000–3,986 BSW4

Knights of the Old Republic—3,964–3,963 BSW4

Jedi vs. Sith—1,000 BSW4

Omnibus: Rise of the Sith—33 BSW4

Episode I: The Phantom Menace—32 BSW4

Omnibus: Emissaries and Assassins—32 BSW4

Twilight—31 BSW4

Bounty Hunters—31 BSW4

The Hunt for Aurra Sing—30 BSW4

Darkness—30 BSW4

The Stark Hyperspace War—30 BSW4

Rite of Passage—28 BSW4

Jango Fett—27 BSW4

Zam Wesell—27 BSW4

Honor and Duty—24 BSW4

Episode II: Attack of the Clones—22 BSW4

Clone Wars—22–19 BSW4

Clone Wars Adventures—22–19 BSW4

General Grievous—22–19 BSW4

Episode III: Revenge of the Sith—19 BSW4

Dark Times—19 BSW4

Omnibus: Droids—5.5 BSW4

Boba Fett: Enemy of the Empire—3 BSW4

Underworld—1 BSW4

Episode IV: A New Hope—SW4

Classic Star Wars—0–3 ASW4

A Long Time Ago . . . —0–4 ASW4

Empire—0 ASW4

Rebellion—0 ASW4

Boba Fett: Man with a Mission—0 ASW4

Omnibus: Early Victories—0–3 ASW4

Jabba the Hutt: The Art of the Deal—1 ASW4

Episode V: The Empire Strikes Back—3 ASW4

Shadows of the Empire—3.5 ASW4

Episode VI: Return of the Jedi—4 ASW4

Mara Jade: By the Emperor's Hand—4 ASW4

Omnibus: X-Wing Rogue Squadron—4–5 ASW4

Heir to the Empire—9 ASW4

Dark Force Rising—9 ASW4

The Last Command—9 ASW4

Dark Empire—10 ASW4

Boba Fett: Death, Lies, and Treachery—10 ASW4

Crimson Empire—11 ASW4

Jedi Academy: Leviathan—12 ASW4

Union—19 ASW4

Chewbacca—25 ASW4

Legacy—130–137 ASW4

Old Republic Era
25,000 – 1000 years before
Star Wars: A New Hope

Rise of the Empire Era
1000 – 0 years before
Star Wars: A New Hope

Rebellion Era
0 – 5 years after
Star Wars: A New Hope

New Republic Era
5 – 25 years after
Star Wars: A New Hope

New Jedi Order Era
25+ years after
Star Wars: A New Hope

Legacy Era
130+ years after
Star Wars: A New Hope

Infinities
Does not apply to timeline

Sergio Aragonés Stomps Star Wars
Star Wars Tales
Star Wars Infinities
Tag and Bink
Star Wars Visionaries

BSW4 = before *Episode IV: A New Hope*. ASW4 = after *Episode IV: A New Hope*.

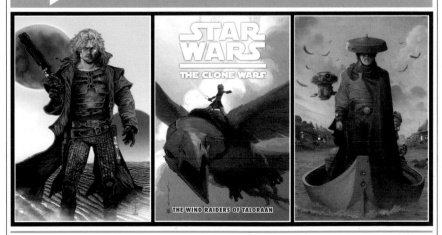

CLONE WARS ADVENTURES

Don't miss any of the action-packed adventures of your favorite **STAR WARS®**
characters, available at comics shops and bookstores in a galaxy near you!

$6.95 each!